Second Edition

Speaking from the *Heart*

Herstories of Chicana, Latina, and Amerindian Women

Rose M. Borunda | Melissa Moreno

Kendall Hunt
publishing company

Kendall Hunt
publishing company

www.kendallhunt.com
Send all inquiries to:
4050 Westmark Drive
Dubuque, IA 52004-1840

Copyright © 2012, 2014 by Rose M. Borunda and Melissa Moreno

ISBN 978-1-4652-4586-1

Printed in the United States of America
10 9 8 7 6 5 4 3 2 1

CONTENTS

ACKNOWLEDGMENTS

We thank Ruth Trinidad, Julie Figueroa, Miroslava Chavez Garcia, Jennie Luna, Anna Kato, Michael Luttropp, and others who provided us with comments. Much appreciation to Linda Anderson for her research related to Rose Borunda's lineage. Also, we thank and honor cultural workers like Gloria Anzaldúa, Paulo Freire, and Elder Mama Cobb, also known as Coxomayotl Xihuatlalli (pronounced Co-sho-mai-yōt See-wot-tlal-li), and others who have inspired and shared their brilliant thinking with us. We dedicate this to our children and their children as well. May they carry on the stories from our ancestors.

INTRODUCTION

Her first step is to take inventory. *Despojando, desgranando, quitando paja.* Just what did she inherit from her ancestors?
—Anzaldúa, 2007, p. 104

As I attempt to take the *his* out of the Chicana [Latina and Amerindian women] story, I am also aware that I too am marked with the history I have inherited. There is no pure, authentic, original history. There are only stories—many stories.
—Perez, 1999, p. xv

At the heart of this book are *her*stories. These are cultural narratives offered by Chicana, Latina, and Amerindian women about how they take different journeys in their effort to decolonize their cultural identity. These narratives are informed by a racialized reality which permeates their daily lives. Some may ask, "What does decolonization mean?" It means first identifying, then interrogating, and finally challenging the unjust practices and demeaning language in our world that creates and normalizes unequal socio-cultural relationships. The process of decolonization does not end here, however. It requires healing from patterns of historical genocide and colonization. These authors not only identify the dehumanizing forces of colonization but they go on to provide ways to negotiate a tension-filled reality in the process of decolonizing while carving out an identity.

The cultural narratives offered by these women express knowledge about how they understand and reclaim their identities. In doing so, they direct their own identity formation. This effort serves as an act of resistance to the universal history that has traditionally negated their existence and knowledge. Furthermore, these *her*stories serve as counter narratives to the "universal" non-multicultural history traditionally taught in U.S. schools and society.

Their process of decolonization does not happen in isolation. These *herstories* are inspired by generations of people communicating and sharing cultural knowledge and folklore. Our ancestors' long legacy provides the deep roots by which women in this collection are not only nurtured but inspired to contest inequalities and evoke change for others. In a journey to eradicate the aftermath of the unjust practices and policies of cultural colonization, these women set out to create a sense of belonging in a U.S. multicultural society.

We, the coauthors, like the contributors, agree that a "universal" history has been represented and taught by a master narrative[1] in primary and secondary schools. This orientation continues to describe and normalize domination. The master narrative is exclusionary to all other perspectives, contributions, and acts of resistance. In and of itself, it is dismissive of any peoples' knowledge, experience, or beliefs that are not aligned with the dominant culture. The master narrative excludes the historical realities of Native and other peoples subjected to colonization and thereby disregards the dignity and humanity of marginalized groups. Subsequently, the dissemination of knowledge from a sole perspective relegates the traditions and perspectives of marginalized groups to a subservient status. As educators, we have heard some of our own college students in Education and Ethnic Studies classes express these very ideas.

The writings of authors who represent voices of marginalized communities are considered counter narratives. Their writings, however, do not constitute the central focus of study in our contemporary primary and secondary schools. Subsequently, their voices are silenced by the educational institutions that have an inclination to predominantly promote a "universal" history. Control of the written word is a privilege as it propagates knowledge in our diverse schools and society; and this privilege can serve as a weapon that subjugates the mind, body, and spirit. Persistent efforts to uphold the written word of privilege are currently evident. In 2010, with Arizona's passage of House Bill 2281, the Tucson Unified School District temporarily banned the Mexican American Studies curriculum and the series of writings offering knowledge of counter narratives. Also in 2013, with the introduction of Senate Bill 1128, the State of Texas proposed that college Ethnic Studies courses would be eliminated as a choice for fulfilling Texas U.S. history requirements. Both

---

[1] In *A Different Mirror: A History of Multicultural America*, Ronald Takaki refers to the master narrative as the inaccurate story that the United States was founded by European Americans (excluding other groups) and that Americans are only white. Takaki indicates that the person who coined this term master narrative was Frederick Jackson in 1893.

of these political efforts were contested by constituencies who resisted being silenced by the master narrative in educational institutions.

We learned from an array of educational scholars and cultural theories that representing cultural narratives requires drawing heavily upon experiential and cultural knowledge that is group- or collective-based (Anzaldúa, 2007; Cantu, 1995; Chabram-Dernersesian, 2007; Freire, 1998; Moraga, 2011; Perez, 1999). Anzaldúa (2007) wrote for "stories to have . . . transformative power, they must arise from the experience of the body in one's own daily life and the metaphors that represent it" (p. 27). She and many others have taught us that a powerful means to communicate cultural knowledge is through the use of a transgressive form of writing, rather than a transparent one. Transgressive writing interweaves multiple voices and bodies of knowledge. This collection of cultural narratives, snapshots of a larger cultural narrative we call *her*stories, is meant to be transgressive in so far as it encourages readers to deconstruct the master narrative and move toward an understanding of the lived realities of those engaged in cultural processes of decolonization.

The coauthors share regional affiliations. Both of our fathers are from the Mesoamerica region and our mothers are from the Southwest region. Our cultural narratives emanate from the experiential and contextual realities of our families negotiating various social, cultural, and political borders. The truths of our *familias* lived realities have allowed us to understand the continuum of oppression resulting from colonization. We draw from the voices of our ancestors in an attempt to connect us to our common cultural heritage.

In this collection, coauthor Borunda offers four cultural narratives that reveal her own trajectory of decolonization. She was born and raised in California's Bay Area, in a Mexican American family. Her family experienced the implications of the U.S.–Mexican War and racial segregation in U.S. society. Borunda left home to attend college in the late 1970s and was among the first generation to immediately benefit from the Civil Rights Act of 1964. Like many of her contemporaries, she experienced the challenges that come with attending a predominantly white educational institution such as the prejudice of her white peers in a slowly racially desegregating society. The value of learning from her "first teachers," Elders in her family and Elders from the wider community, became major sources of inspiration in her life. Her early professional experiences in the child abuse prevention field and additional years serving as a public school counselor fueled her commitment to social justice.

Within Borunda's four narratives, elements of cultural struggle, human agency, and resilience are evident. Each story, contextualized within a period of time, demonstrates the connectedness of "self" to a rich heritage of resistance to domination. The first story, entitled, "Cultivating a Seed of Consciousness," provides a reflection on the experience of resisting the forces of cultural hegemony and racialized messages. In Chapter 2, she explores "Differentiated Realities in Mexico," the interrelationship of the two sides of her family who, despite their separate and oppositional positions in Mexican society, converge to create a new and emerging cultural identity. In the narrative in Chapter 3, "Violence, Love, and Spanish Colonialism," she portrays parallel existences shared by her paternal grandparents and her maternal grandmother to reveal the values inherent within the racial and class hierarchy. The converging forces of conquest and colonization impact the very nature of who Borunda is today. "Regeneration" in Chapter 4 speaks to her active interrogation of colonization while drawing upon Indigenous practices in an effort to promote her healing and to regenerate an identity informed by her own set of standards, rather than one defined by others. Through this effort, she confronts historical lies and discovers truths that replace them. In doing so, Borunda deflects the impact of symbolic violence. The desire for liberation and the joy of attaining it are central to her journey. Collectively, these cultural narratives represent and honor the accumulative effort of those who came before us and who, in their own way, fought to retain their physical, spiritual, and cultural dignity as well as a sense of belonging in spite of years of colonization.

Each of Borunda's four cultural narratives is preceded by a short context offered by coauthor Moreno. Like Borunda, Moreno was born and raised in California. In San Joaquin Valley's Westside, her mother constantly reminded her that her Indigenous family had lived in the Southwest for over 500 years, while her father taught her that this land was once Mexican. By drawing on secondary historical texts, oral history, and folklore, Moreno provides a description of discourses and practices about domination and resistance that shape identity formations of Chicana, Latina, and Amerindian communities across various eras. Chapter discussion questions and resources are also included in the last section of this text to facilitate analytical and reflective discussions about power, inequality, and epistemology, as well as resistance and resilience of marginalized people.

Concluding the book is a distinctive and moving collection of cultural narratives,[2] *her*stories. By drawing on their experiential knowledge, Jennie

---

[2] The contexts and cultural narratives throughout this book include Spanish words that are not translated and not always italicized, unless there is an emphasis for the purpose of expressing bilingual and bicultural sensibilities and dispositions. Knowledge of Spanish language can be easily accessible through a Spanish language dictionary or on the internet.

Luna, Cindy Cruz, Julie Figueroa, Maria Mejorado, Michelle Maher, Angie Chabram, Rebecca Rosa, Sofia Villenas, Margarita Berta-Avila, Caroline Sotello Viernes Turner, Ruth Trinidad-Galván, and Marcela S. Jáuregui, together, offer cultural narratives about their struggles toward decolonization and the practices and discourses they engage in order to form a sense of belonging in this society. As Anzaldúa (2007) would put it, they "take inventory" of what they have inherited from their ancestors (p. 104) that can aid them in their cultural process of decolonization. Each of their cultural narratives is undergirded by a unique voice rooted in their own identity formation and web of relationships. These contributors have dedicated their lives to Education and Ethnic Studies and their stories, as a collective, represent a diverse dialog about our subjectivity in a multicultural society. This collective of *her*stories portrays the connections of people whose ancestry has persisted and existed on this land or hemisphere for thousands of years. These interrelationships transcend borders and laws that divide people from one another. The common sensibilities, desires, and struggles of these women, including the coauthors, provide the potential to engage one another, from the heart, to create a more just and inclusive world.

The series of cultural narratives and discussion questions in this collection are intended to help in the deconstruction of the master narrative and to serve various educational purposes, including explaining identity formations. Following in the tradition of Freire (1998), who challenged the tenants of "banking education" as the act of depositing information from teacher to student, we encourage readers to: (1) engage in a critical examination of previously held beliefs and teachings about the self and culture(s), (2) unveil states of subversion within a reality that is constructed by others in power, and (3) develop the capacity to understand the essence of subjectivity and the capacity to reexamine one's positionality in the world. For us, engaging in these processes of critical reflection has meant embracing instances of empowerment and claiming expressions of voice in schools, culture, and society. Through our cultural narratives, we invite our readers to critically reflect on their own narrative.

References

Anzaldúa, G. (2007). *Borderlands/la frontera: The new Mestiza* (3rd ed.). San Francisco, CA: Aunt Lute.

Cantu, N. E. (1995). *Canicula: Snapshots of a girlhood en la frontera.* Albuquerque, NM: University of New Mexico Press.

Chabram-Dernersesian, A. (2007). *The Chicana/o cultural studies forum: Critical and ethnographic practices.* New York and London: New York University Press.

Freire, P. (1998). *Pedagogy of the oppressed.* New York: The Continuum Publishing Company.

Moraga, C. L. (2011). *A Xicana codex of changing consciousness: Writings, 2000–2010.* Durham, NC: Duke University Press.

Perez, E. (1999). *The decolonial imaginary: Writing Chicanas into history.* Bloomington, IN: Indiana University Press.

1

An Anglo-Mexican American Context

Negotiating violence a sense of belonging in schools and society is central to coming of age. Borunda's narrative focuses on the resiliency and struggle to belong that is challenged by historically limiting policies and racial prejudice. Narratives about the struggle for Mexican Americans to belong in the U.S. society began in 1848, with the ending of what was once Mexico in the Southwest and California regions. However, long before 1848, the lands were Native. Through multiple forces of domination and genocidal violence, Native peoples were stripped of their land by the Spaniards beginning in 1521, by the Mexicans in 1821, and then by Anglo settlers in 1848. Patterns of violence and land displacement intensified during the U.S. Westward Expansion and Gold Rush that brought massive numbers of immigrants to the Southwest and California. Subsequently, Native and Mexican people lost claim to all of their resources including social and political protection (Almaguer, 1994; Heidenreich, 2007; Menchaca, 1995).

In 1848, the war between the United States and Mexico ended with the Treaty of Guadalupe Hidalgo, which theoretically promised that Mexicans residing north of the U.S.–Mexican border would gain U.S. citizenship and maintain their land, language, and religion. In practice, applying the Treaty was nearly impossible even for Mexican elites that were known as Californios. English-speaking legal officials favored Anglo Americans in ongoing disputes concerning land, livestock, rivers, and other resources (Camarillo, 1979; Gutierrez, 1991). In California, according to Latta (1980), "in one great robbery that stripped central coast rancheros of most of their horses, all were taken from pioneer Californios" (p. 35). There were wide-scale attacks on Mexicans with the intent of running them out of certain counties such as Calaveras County and Amador County. The means by which these movements were enacted was through public humiliation or death. Castillo and Camarillo (1973) state that during this period, "Mexicans were lynched, flogged, branded, and ultimately driven from their claims by force" (p. 35). Along with being dispossessed of their lands, U.S. Mexicans were relegated to low-paying jobs and also faced discriminatory policies created by Anglo Americans (Almaguer, 1994; Heidenreich, 2007; Menchaca, 1995). For example, among the early policies that impacted the socioeconomic and political status of Mexicans and Mexican Americans in California were the Foreigner Miners Tax Law of 1852 and the Greaser Act of 1855.

The Foreigner Miners Tax Law intended to criminalize foreigners that mined gold, and in this process, Mexicans (as well as Chinese) were highly profiled. Resistance to the mistreatment brought a backlash that included having their families murdered. Such was the case of Joaquin Murieta. According to folklore, Murieta was a miner whose gold claim was stolen by gold-greedy Anglos that whipped him, hanged his brother, and raped his wife in his presence. The enraged Murieta then focused his life to avenge his family's honor by bringing death to Anglo officials for not addressing the violence his family and he experienced (Meire & Ribera, 1993). As described, the conflict between the Anglo and Mexican miners undoubtedly elevated the painting of Joaquin as the "bloody bandit." Murieta's actions were those of a man who retaliated against the oppression of Mexicans; "he was an avenger against the conquering Anglos" (Castillo & Camarillo, p. 35). Murieta and other social bandits—like Tiburcio Vasquez, Elfego Baca, Juan Cortina, Gregorio Cortez, and others—fought back. On one hand, these Mexican men were identified as "bloody bandits" to those in power, and on the other hand, to U.S. Mexicans, they became symbols of resistance against the Anglo-dominating economic and political system.

Anti-Mexican hostility was also articulated in the Greaser Act. This was an anti-Mexican law that indicated that anyone of Spanish and Indian "blood," that was armed, and that was outspoken would be branded a criminal. The implications of this policy, like the Foreigner Miners Tax Law, legitimized the idea that anyone of Mexican descent was a potential threat and was subsequently labeled a bandit (Rosenbaum, 1981; Vigil, 2012). In their own respective regions, Mexican social bandits disputed racist policies and asserted their right to land, livestock, and use of public spaces (Camarillo, 1979). They did this in the face of multiple forms of domination such as the threat of public lynching. Among those lynched were men named Joaquin, Tiburcio Vasquez, and even of a woman named Juanita. In 1851, in Downieville, California, Juanita was the first Mexican woman lynched by a mob after she defended herself from Fredrick Cannon, who harassed her. Displays of Mexican decapitated heads at state fairs were not uncommon (Guidotti-Hernandez, 2011). These public representations of discipline and punishment served as a means to intimidate the Mexican population from resisting the new structure. According to Menchaca (1995), "Violent actions committed against Mexicans ranged from police brutality to Ku Klux Klan intimidation. Although police brutality was the most common form of violence, Mexicans on occasion were suspiciously and accidently maimed by 'law-abiding' Anglo American citizens" (p. 46). These practices of domination and racist policies served to promote the idea that Mexicans were "strangers in their own land" throughout the 1800s (Takaki, 1993).

Along with becoming strangers in their own land, U.S. Mexicans also contended with being identified as foreigners and were deported under the policies of the Mexican Repatriation Act in the 1930s and Operation Wetback in 1953. The Mexican Repatriation Act was put into motion during the Great Depression. This was a time when a monopoly took place among U.S. financial agencies adversely affecting the overall national political economy, yet Mexicans were identified as the scapegoat. This policy sanctioned three practices; the roundups and physical removal of Mexican people, announcements offering free transportation to Mexico, and the termination of social services to Mexican families. Between 1932 and 1938, about 100,000 Mexicans were repatriated, including U.S. born, across the border on trains destined for Mexico (Meier & Ribera, 1993). Operation Wetback was another massive deportation drive approved by the Attorney General's office that was intended to discourage employers from hiring undocumented workers. During this time, many Americans and the government viewed Mexican workers as a threat to U.S. labor. Together, the Mexican Repatriation Act and Operation Wetback impacted U.S. and non–U.S. born Mexicans' citizenship and their sense of belonging in U.S. society.

In response to practices of racial discrimination and segregation in schools and society, there began an emergence of associations and organizations throughout the 1900s (Sanchez, 1993) such as the League of United Latin American Citizens (LULAC), which was formed in 1929.

Americanization

This organization was founded in Corpus Christi, Texas, and it "promoted an understanding of Mexican Americans as American citizens foremost" (Oropeza, 2005, p. 18). LULAC become active during the Great Depression (Kaplowitz 2005) and it refuted the massive deportation of Mexicans that was promoted by the Mexican Repatriation Act. LULAC, and other civic organizations sought to "Americanize" the U.S.–Mexican population and also to counter some of the ideas that were undergirded by the Eugenics Movement. Eugenics officials claimed to improve the human species, particularly with respect to hereditary qualities and race. Eugenics officials intended to address population control, and in this process, they deemed nonwhite populations as inferior in intelligence. Eugenics programs promoted the sterilization of populations that were nonwhite, were disabled, or otherwise deemed inferior, including Mexican American women (Gutiérrez, 2008; Nourse, 2008). Ideas and practices rooted in Eugenics that began around 1910 were contested long after World War II.

Toward the end of World War II in 1945, Mexican Americans that had served in the U.S. military returned to find that racial discrimination, segregation, and their inferior status in society continued. Mexican Americans also found that the government had implemented the Bracero Guest Worker Program, from 1942 to 1964. This program imported a large number of Mexican nationals to work for less pay in the same jobs that Mexican Americans had traditionally occupied. The surplus of Mexican labor did not change the patterns of racial discrimination in the employment, housing, and educational sectors for Mexican Americans. In response to the racial discrimination and conditions of poverty, Mexican American veterans created the GI Forum organization, which joined forces with LULAC, in order to file legal cases to challenge racial discrimination and segregation in schools, society, and in the labor force (Garcia, 1989). In 1947, they were successful in the legal case of Mendez vs. Westminster that took place in Southern California. This case challenged the racial segregation of Mexican and Mexican American children in several schools. Ultimately, this case became fundamental for the 1954 landmark case Brown vs. Board of Education, which called for national desegregation efforts in public schools.

While there were attempts to desegregate schools, the employment sector lagged far behind. The United Farm Workers (UFW) officially emerged in 1962 as the primary organization to address the inequality in the Mexican American farm labor sector (Ross, 1989). Its major focus was on improving farm worker wages, working conditions, housing, and labor equipment. By 1964, cofounder of the UFW, Cesar Chavez, and UFW supporter Dr. Ernesto Galarza managed to meet with the U.S. Congress for the elimination of the Bracero Guest Worker Program. Chavez and Galarza argued that the surplus labor created by the Program had a detrimental impact on the U.S. Mexican population testifying that prevailing conditions could not improve their poor education, poor housing conditions, and other social issues of inequality. They also argued that the poor wages and working conditions of the Braceros created overwhelming and long-lasting health and poverty issues among farm workers.

These concerns were expressed during the emergence of a new generation among the Mexican Americans that created the Chicano Movement. This was during the Vietnam War era (Oropeza, 2005). The movement included labor, land, educational, and feminist demands (Blackwell, 2011). In particularly, due to the passage of the 1964 Civil Rights Act, the educational segment of the Chicano Movement made demands. They included the need to access college preparation courses and increase the availability of Mexican American history courses, Mexican American teachers, and Chicano Studies programs (Donato, 1997; Munoz, 2007; Urrieta, 2009). Prior to the passage of the 1964 Civil Rights Act, most public and private institutions in society could summarily exclude nonwhite populations and not suffer any consequence for discriminatory practices. As a result of protests for equality and equity, there was a call for an "affirmative action" to create diversity in higher sectors of employment and higher education. Post-Civil Rights, Chicanos/as and Latinas/os continue the struggle for equal schooling, a sense of belonging, citizenship (Flores & Benmayor, 1997; Moreno, 2008), and for citizenship reform.

References

Almaguer, T. (1994). *Racial fault lines: The historical origins of white supremacy in California.* Berkeley, CA: University of California Press.

Blackwell, M. (2011). *¡Chicana Power! Contested histories of feminism in the Chicano movement.* Austin, TX: University of Texas Press.

Camarillo, A. C. (1979). *Chicanos in a changing society: From Mexican pueblos to American barrios in Santa Barbara and Southern California, 1848–1930.* Cambridge, MA: Harvard University Press.

Castillo, P., & Camarillo, A. (1973). *Furia y muerte: Los banditos Chicanos. Aztlan,* 4, 1–167.

Donato, R. (1997). *The other struggle for equal schools: Mexican American during the Civil Rights Era.* New York, NY: State University of New York Press.

Flores, W. V., & Benmayor, R. (1997). *Latino cultural citizenship: Claiming identity, space, and rights.* Boston, MA: Beacon Press.

Garcia, M. T. (1989). *Mexican Americans: Leadership, ideology, & identity 1930–1960.* New Haven, CT, & London: Yale University Press.

Guidotti-Hernandez, N. (2011). *Unspeakable violence: Narratives of mourning and loss in Chicana/o and US Mexico national imaginaries.* Durham, NC: Duke University Press.

Gutiérrez, E. R. (2008). *Fertile matters: The politics of Mexican-origin women's reproduction.* Austin, TX: University of Texas Press.

Heidenreich, L. (2007). *'This land was Mexican once': Histories of resistance from Northern California.* Austin, TX: University of Texas Press.

Kaplowitz, C. A. (2005). *LULAC Mexican Americans and national policy.* College Station, TX: Texas A&M University Press.

Menchaca, M. (1995). *The Mexican outsiders: A community history of marginalization and discrimination in California.* Austin, TX: University of Texas Press.

Moreno, M. (2008). Citizenship surveillance of la gente (people): Theory, practice, research and cultural citizen voices. *Social Justice: A Journal of Crime, Conflict, and World Order* 35(1): 1–5.

Munoz, C. (2007). *Youth, identity, and power: The Chicano movement.* London: Verso Books.

Nourse, V. F. (2008). *In reckless hands: Skinner v. Oklahoma and the near-triumph of American Eugenics.* New York, NY: WW Norton and Company.

Oropeza, L. (2005). *¡Raza si! ¡Guerra no!: Chicano protest and patriotism during the Viet Nam WAR era.* Berkeley, CA: University of California Press.

Rosenbaum, R. (1981). *Mexicano resistance in the Southwest.* Dallas, TX: Southern Methodist University Press.

Ross, F. (1989). *Cesar Chavez at the beginning: Conquering Goliath.* Keene, CA: An El Taller Grafico Press Book.

Sanchez, G. J. (1993). *Becoming Mexican American: Ethnicity, culture and identity in Chicano Los Angeles, 1900–1945.* New York, NY: Oxford University Press.

Takaki, R. (1993). *A different mirror: A history of multicultural America.* Boston, MA: Little, Brown and Company.

Urrieta, L. Jr. (2009). *Working from within: Chicana and Chicano activist educators in Whitestream schools.* Tucson, AZ: University of Arizona Press.

Vigil, J. D. (2012). *From Indians to Chicano: The dynamic of Mexican American culture* (3rd ed.). Long Grove, IL: Waveland Press, Inc.

NARRATIVE 1: *CULTIVATING A SEED OF CONSCIOUSNESS*

Even before I got to high school, I remember holding within me the malignant seed of anger but not knowing how it got there, what made it sprout, and why it was growing. It, as well as that which made the seed flourish, became a part of me. Throughout my elementary and middle school years,

It all seemed very normal.

Each day, starting with elementary school, was as ordinary as the last. I left my home for school every morning with lunch pail in hand. My mother would make a fresh bologna sandwich and include a Twinkie, Ho Ho or cupcake, and a piece of fruit. My classmates and I would trade our sweets during lunch break. If the fruit was an apple or orange, it held minimal negotiation value but bananas, bruised, and mushy after bouncing around the inside of the lunch pail all morning were hard to pass off.

My route from home to the bus stop took me through a nursery that contained endless rows of miniature trees and plants. It did not matter that the plants were in pots ranging from one to five gallons and that some only stood a foot and a half high. As I was generally smaller in stature compared to my peers, I imagined the trees to be gigantic redwoods towering above my petite frame. I would stand in the midst of the vegetation and marvel at their size, their textures, and fragrances that filled the morning air.

Arriving safely and on time to catch the big yellow school bus that carried me off to school required physical agility and mental cunning on my part; the maze of potted plants and trees transformed into a luscious forest and presented illusory threats. Nonetheless, I prevailed every morning having escaped the imaginary perils that existed in my fantasy forest. With lunch pail in hand, I arrived at the designated bus stop, unharmed, and stood in line with the other kids from our rural neighborhood. As we rode the big yellow bus a few miles down the road to the public schools, we observed the rising sun bathe the eastern face of Mt. Diablo.

My father left for work before my brother and I were awake but evidence that he had been up before us hung in the air—the smell of fresh brewed coffee and the breakfast prepared by my mother. His lunch, too, had been carefully packed in his lunch pail that morning. He often worked double shifts at the steel mill in the East Bay Area and also worked weekends driving tractor for local farmers. Alterations of the earth over thousands of years made it possible for him to do both.

We lived on the eastern outskirts of the San Francisco Bay Area where it bordered the San Joaquin Valley. In ancient times, the San Joaquin Valley was under a sea. Shifts of the land made it so that the sea lost its' waters that receded into the ocean but left behind fertile land for farming. Deep channel waterways such as the Sacramento and San Joaquin Rivers eventually connected the ocean to the communities that would rise from this ancient sea floor; a multitude of harbors for commerce placed along the way. Steel was one of the commodities to be exported from the port of Pittsburg, California, the destination to which my father drove his truck every morning under a blanket of stars. This, he did, hours before I studied the peak of a mountain, once an island in the time when water covered the land, as I was carried down the road in a big yellow bus. Despite not seeing our father for stretches of days, my brother and I understood that his labor was imprinted upon the landscape.

My mother worked seasonally at a nearby tomato cannery. When I was old enough to carry a miniature-sized bucket, I joined my parents and one and only sibling, my brother Henry Jr., in the fields. I wasn't much help though. My brother tells me I ate more than what I added to the family effort. His memory attests to my lack of productivity; he would be working his way down a row of tomatoes and then realize that I hadn't been by his side for quite some time. On his return to the large wooden crates to empty his tomato-filled bucket, he'd find me sheltered in the shade of the containers. My little bucket lay empty beside me. One hand held a shaker of salt and the other held a freshly picked tomato, a big bite missing. He said I wasn't all that discrete as tomato juice covered my face.

Somehow, I figured out early in life that working in the fields would not be the best vocation for me. I had no idea what I would do with my life because as a child, one does not generally give much consideration to the future but I had learned, from experience and observation, that farm work was hard. It was physically hard and taxing on the body. The short hoe was preferred by farmers because its use by farm workers minimized damage to valuable crops. While the plants were spared, the backs and knees of our family and of other people who worked in the fields, were not. Complaints of chronic and sometimes crippling pain were widespread. I internalized very early in my life that our bodies were expendable, of less value than the crops we picked.

The messages of "less worth" were prevalent. For example, my brother told me how he had befriended a boy who lived in one of the migrant farm worker camps close to our home. He and the other boy had agreed to meet at the camp one day as it was only a bike ride away. On his way to the camp down a dirt road, my brother came across a pallet with cartons stacked one upon the other. It was about six feet high. The cans were clearly marked as dog food. My brother recalled looking around and thinking, "Where are the dogs?" He said it, "Creeped him out." Later, the stories came out of how the local farmer was taking labels off of wet canned dog food and giving them to people living in the migrant farm worker camp. The lowered value of human beings and their mistreatment was such that. . .

It was considered normal, by some.

I was never ashamed that I worked in the fields. It taught me discipline and gave me an appreciation for the hard effort it took to put food on the table. I also developed a sense of camaraderie with the children of other families who labored alongside us. I lacked, however, the sustained focus to one task. My mind easily wandered. It didn't take much for me to get distracted and before long I would be eating what I was supposed to be collecting or would be engrossed in creative amusement. For example, during walnut season, I found great sport in throwing dirt clods at nearby targets, my brother, birds, shadows, to pass the time. I partially credit this experience as furthering my skill as a budding softball player.

Nonetheless, staying focused in school, during the 1960s and 1970s, drew different challenges. I'd breeze through the workbooks and dittos provided by my teachers, finishing them before the majority of my classmates. To pass the time, I'd fidget with my pencil, then, much to the dismay of the teacher, I would try to distract my classmates. After a stern look or two from the teacher, I would turn to other entertainment such as the shiny linoleum classroom floor that appeared much like the ice-skating rinks I had seen on the television. I had developed ice-skating skills during the winter season. The dirt road that we lived on had many potholes that accumulated water after a heavy rain. In the freezing temperatures of the early morning, the water froze and provided the perfect surface to slide across as I made the trek to the bus stop. Observing my classmates still toiling over their worksheet, I would get up from my desk and sashay across the floor like Peggy Fleming, the Olympic ice-skater. Given my small stature, I had a lower center of gravity so could slide with incredible balance and grace. I thought I was pretty good but my teacher wasn't so impressed.

My ice-skating skills and dirt clod throwing accuracy didn't account for much at the time. The following year, third grade, I was placed in a class that contained a raucous group of kids who were either low-income white or of Mexican descent like me. We got along relatively well, but I found it odd that we had separate recess times from the two other third grade classes. Their classrooms were located opposite one another and down the hall from us. Those students would go back and forth to each other's classes and do cooperative activities. We didn't interact much with the kids in those classes even though I knew some of them. This familiarity stemmed from the various interactions between our respective families. My family worked the land that their parents owned.

My third grade teacher, a first year teacher, was one of two male teachers at our elementary school. Over the year, the teacher developed impeccable crowd control skills. The only time I can remember where things got *too* out of control was the day one of my classmates fell out of the classroom window. Luckily, it was just a one-story drop. I am still not sure why this classmate was perched on the window sill and I will, most likely, never know. Later, when we were in high school, this kid married another classmate. Both, Mexican Americans, supposedly went missing along with his wife's younger sister. Rumor had it that they were involved in a drug deal that went bad and their bodies were tucked in one of the stacked and crushed cars at a local auto wrecker business.

These are the kind of tales concocted to explain life outcomes that were inconceivable to those of us who were trying to imagine something more promising for our own. Incomplete life stories do not stand alone so preclude us from measuring our own lives against them. Urban legends, with their tragic conclusions, provide a period to the end of the story. I like to think that this former third grade classmate, his wife, and sister-in-law slipped away from the violent situation just like he slipped out of the classroom window because other than an occasional fight with the teacher or falling out a window, this classmate's behavior was not much out of the ordinary.

It was all normal.

The one classmate that most of us avoided in third grade was the kid who smelled bad. He was one of the few white kids in class. His parents owned a business downtown. We couldn't figure out why they couldn't get him to bathe. My classmates and I spent the year devising ways to avoid sitting next to him in class. His family's business didn't do well. They packed up and moved at the end of the school year; the building where their business stumbled to a halt had an "Available for Lease" sign posted at the front window. That marked the end, for us third graders, of having to avoid the boy who didn't bathe. It never occurred to me, when I was a child that this family was struggling and did not have the resources; including a full bathroom in the store from which they tried to scrape a living, while also living in it.

I apparently impressed the third grade teacher who mastered keeping kids from falling out of windows. The next year, I was placed with the only other male teacher in our school where I could experience fourth grade with some of the kids from the other two third grade classes. Much to my delight, we were given access to self-paced assignments that I whizzed through without having to wait for my classmates. Getting out of the chair to pick out the next assignment was sanctioned. It gave me an excuse to move and it made it easier to keep my butt in the seat because my mind was repeatedly engaged in grasping new material.

In fifth grade, I was placed in a class that was a split fourth and fifth grade class. I was not sure if the fourth graders in this class were so smart that they were placed with us fifth graders for an accelerated experience or that us fifth graders were considered so slow that we were in a class that was a step above being retained; kind of like purgatory. This was the year that I memorized and recited the Gettysburg address; perfectly delivered to my classmates, word for word. I did not understand the meaning of the words and without context for phrases such as, ". . . dedicated to the proposition that all men are created equal" the words floated in the air above the heads of my fourth and fifth grade classmates who looked equally clueless as to what I was saying.

After working my classmates' parents' fields on weekends and summers, then sharing recess time on the playground, we, the children of farm workers and the children of farmers, got used to sharing some of the same spaces; sports teams, bands, and choirs. My father's parents, Mama Lupé and Papa José, attended one of my first music concerts, he wearing his sombrero and she a reboso draped across her shoulders. My beginning band played a rousing rendition of "Mary Had a Little Lamb." I played extra loud to make sure that my grandparents heard me. I don't think that my music teacher appreciated my robust volume. During the performance, he kept motioning to me with the palm of his hand to tone it down. Afterward, I ran to the guest seating and my Papa José gave me a big hug. I was glad I had played extra loud.

My one and only brother is several years older than me. We were a dwarf of a family compared to my uncles' and aunts' families on my dad's side. They had large families so that older cousins attended the local high school with my brother. This was during the tail end of the Civil Rights Era. Mexican American students were actively involved in the Chicano Movement and wrote poems in "Raza Newsletters" about having Brown Pride. The fact that people were proud of being brown was confusing to me. My mother always told me to cover my head whenever I was outside for fear that I would get darker than I already was. I was not born with her naturally fair skin; instead, I was the earth tones of my Mama Lupé and Papa José.

My brother brought home Raza Newsletters and I would read the poems written and published by high school Chicano students. The words of one poem stuck with me. It was something akin to, ". . . if people who were 'white' thought they were 'right' then they should stay out of sight." I remember those words because I thought the author was very clever in her use of rhyme.

The raging taking place in the world around me was difficult to understand as an elementary and then a middle school student. We did not actively participate in walkouts nor were we encouraged to boldly demonstrate our "Brown Pride." Nonetheless, when I accompanied my mother to the grocery store, I knew we were not supposed to buy grapes because of the boycott that Cesar Chavez and the United Farm Workers had asked all to support. Unintentionally but yet almost instinctively, I expressed solidarity with the movements. I wore my pride, literally; my feet bore the leather of moccasins and my hair was braided like an *India*. Around my neck, I donned colorful beads and my clothing reflected the deep colors of purples and reds with contrasts of black or white. My ethnic identification was overtly stated through my very presence. I listened to music from Santana, El Chicano, and Malo *a todo dar*. And, to reflect alliance with other souls of the era whose lyrics gave voice to the times, there was even Sly and the Family Stone, Janis Joplin, and Jimmy Hendrix in the musical mix. So, with lyrics to "Purple Haze" repeating in my head, I would spend weekend nights at Mexican dances and watch my parents glide across the dance floor to *corridos*. In these spaces, there was no need to aggressively demonstrate pride, we just lived it.

While in middle school, a number of students in our grade were tested for the Gifted and Talented Education (GATE) program. None of my Chicanita friends nor I qualified for the program and we did not find it odd or question, at the time, that the kids whose parents were farm owners, teachers, or administrators did. After the results were announced, they went on field trips to the City (San Francisco) and who knows what other privileges were given to these individuals who had demonstrated intellectual superiority because,

This all seemed to be a normal and natural outcome.

While this select group left on the bus for a day in the City, my Chicanita friends and I stayed behind and worked on our English vocabulary. This being the reason I didn't qualify; my knowledge of English was insufficient compared to my classmates who spoke only English. I found the standard of measurement odd because had those kids been given that entire exam *en español*. . . . Well, *imagine*. We were already accustomed to having separate spaces even in shared places such as school so it was not unusual for us to stay behind and watch the bus leave for the City. This conveyed to us, once again, that this would be one of those separate spaces in which we had not qualified ourselves to be.

At home, my father enforced that we speak only Spanish. That was the language with which I communicated in the warm and welcome spaces of my home with, my Mama Lupé and Papa Jose, and with my Grandma Salcido, my mother's mother. At school, the use of Spanish incited dirty looks even if it was during recess. My Spanish-speaking friends and I were well aware that our older siblings had been subjected to physical punishment for speaking the language in public school. In those days, the use of corporal punishment was still employed in schools. Our principal kept a big paddle hanging on the wall of his office to enact punishment for our crime of speaking this forbidden language.

My friends and I complied with the unwritten rule in public spaces but we spoke *Spanish* as an act of resistance beyond range of the yard duty supervisor's *orejas*. Knowing that we would be physically punished for speaking a language that marked us as Mexican was a clear message, but it wasn't as if not speaking it minimized the fact that whether we spoke it or not, we were still ethnically, Mexican. It made me wonder if physical violence was being used to eliminate our use of a language, how much more would be employed to minimize that which made us products of our heritage. The forces of ethnic elimination constantly served as a reminder that our presence was often, at best, tolerated, and often unwelcome. My brother was reminded of this when he would get picked on at the bus stop by the neighborhood bully, a white kid. My brother's crime for which he was thrown up against and then pinned to the wall of a building by our bus stop was restated to him with absolute clarity. As the bully held my brother up against the wall with his hands around his throat, the bully would remind him that the mistreatment was warranted for *"being Mexican."*

This all was normal. This is just the way it was.

While people were fed dog food and my brother avoided the taunts of the neighborhood bully, a group called the Youngbloods' lyrics spoke to our generation through our transistor radios, "Come on people now, smile on your brother, everybody get together, try to love one another right now."

Our reality was filled with contradictions.

Somewhere between the somewhat shared spaces, the separate spaces, and the spaces in between where dirty looks and threats of violence took place, the anger in me grew. It wasn't as if I could ever say that I was summarily dismissed and mistreated but I perceived the unequal treatment between white and nonwhite students. Contradictions in what the nation was striving to be and what our day-to-day reality continued to be tainted perceptions. Overall, it was subtle behavior detected from interactions as I stepped into the public domain. My anger must have been evident to others because I was referred to the school psychologist who happened to be of Mexican descent. One day, the anger slipped out in the form of a cuss word and I was sent to the Principal. I got the paddle for it. All I could say to myself about that was, *"Si quiera no me descubrieron hablando español!"* While my proficiency in the sully side of English vocabulary was unwelcome, I knew that the use of Spanish was a greater infraction.

While learning the rules of shared spaces in the public domain, I continued to do well in academics. This was made possible by the fact that I always enjoyed learning. My Grandma Salcido had instilled in me that a formal education was something that one should acquire and that once you had knowledge, no one could take it away. She had the benefit of a formal education, up to eighth grade which by standards of her era, was a privilege. Having it made a difference during critical junctures in her life. She impressed upon me her faith that an education would make a difference for me though she had no idea what the future would hold.

One of the most monumental gifts my mother gave me was a library card. The County Library was in a converted home in the center of town. It was, at most, 800 square feet but because each book on its shelves opened the world to me, I was able to travel on story lines that took me to faraway places. I was a voracious reader and delighted in the stories, pictures, and experiences that spoke through words on the pages. This was an outlet that tantalized my mind and imagination. Even then, I recognized the power of the written word.

Outside of my circle of Chicanita friends, there were classmates and teachers who made the experience of school more welcoming and less "schizoid making." They felt like exceptions to the indifferent and sometimes animosity filled reality. Even though those a generation ahead of me had fought for the right to be *equal* within the school system, I struggled, at times, to keep myself mentally engaged for even though we shared equal space, we were not always looked upon as *equals*. In the thick of this gray area that Lincoln and his contemporaries had attempted to cleanse, I found the exceptional teachers, secretaries, cafeteria workers, and friends who greeted me with sincere smiles and open hearts. Then, I struggled to keep my behavior "in check" in the spaces where I felt like an *arrimada*.

Expanded Spaces

At the end of our eighth grade year, the high school counselors came to our middle school and met with each and every incoming freshman for one-on-one sessions. This meeting was intended to prepare us for our upcoming high school years. My family had taught me to be *bien educada* so compliantly I went at the appointed time to meet with the woman who would be my high school counselor for the next four years of my academic career. To my amazement, she was as petite as I was. She was Chilean, spoke Spanish, and was not afraid to speak it out loud which I found to be bold and made me immediately respect her even more.

From a pile of folders stacked on the table in between us, she pulled out a folder that appeared to be thicker than most of the others. Each folder held student academic and behavioral records. She opened the folder and began to review the contents. Whatever it was she was reading made her eyebrows arch like a rainbow. She quickly closed the folder as though trying to contain the information from spilling out into the room itself and ensuring that I didn't spy upon the contents. She regarded the closed folder for a silent moment, looked at me long and hard, and then said, "You are going to be placed in honors College Prep classes."

I said, "That's fine." I got up and returned to my class wondering, "What is College?" and furthermore, what does the "honors" part mean? This was 1973. While I understood that these courses would prepare me for something after high school, I had no concept of what that meant. My list of options for my future already eliminated field work as I lacked the aptitude. A few of my older male cousins were serving the U.S. military and fighting in Vietnam, but the roles for women at this time in the military were limited so, again, options were uncertain.

Being in honors College Prep classes meant being with the kids who had been in one of the two other third-grade classes and even those who later took the San Francisco field trip on the GATE bus. To my surprise, I discovered that they weren't necessarily smarter than me or my classmates from the class where the boy fell out of the window. I often helped them with their homework and some often cheated off of me on tests. It was all fun though because my social circle suddenly expanded. Once I began to share the academic spaces with a different range of classmates, I began to hang out more with people who participated in athletics, music, drama, and journalism. These were activities that had appeal to me as well. The shared interests introduced me to a world of engagement at school with teachers who were inviting and kind. An incredible music teacher from elementary school, Mr. Geddes, had first placed a trumpet in my hands. His high school successor, Mr. Jones, continued to foster my love of music and performing everything from classical to Latin jazz. My tomboy days of playing baseball with my brother along with my dirt clod throwing days in the orchards finally paid off. I made the softball team where my ability to throw objects with accuracy was sanctioned. I even ran for class office and became freshman class secretary. The world opened up and I started to feel more of what can only be described as *acceptance.*

During my freshman year, my counselor called me in to her office. She told me that there was a university that offered scholarships to minority students who were involved in school extracurricular activities and who maintained a high grade point average. My brother was attending a community college and I had visited the University of California, Berkeley campus, earlier in the year with my marching band, so learned, firsthand, what college was.

Despite the fact that Patty Hearst, heiress to a major American publishing empire, had been kidnapped from her apartment in Berkeley and the kidnappers, the Symbionese Liberation Army (SLA), was negotiating food for needy families of California in exchange for the heiress, I was unfazed. After watching UC Berkeley's Marching Band high step across the field with sousaphones swaying side to side, I envisioned myself marching across a college football field with thousands watching. The idea enthralled me. This made me decide that, yes, I would go to college. I snapped out of my daydream as I realized that my counselor was waiting for a response. I acceded to her offer; I would continue to stay in college preparatory classes and remain active in extracurricular activities. I saw nothing wrong with the actions of the SLA. They were modern day Robin Hoods in an era in which anger over generational injustice was evident everywhere.

At the time, despite seeing the images from our television of people being attacked by police forces with German Shepard dogs, batons, blaring water from fire hoses, I drew no correlation between myself and Brown vs. Board of Education. Such landmark decisions resulting from the Civil Rights Era felt as distant and removed as the words I had recited in fifth grade when I said, ". . . all men are created equal." Yet, despite the fact that I was growing up in the shadow of this Era, the gains made were such that,

Suddenly, there was an emerging new normal.

Throughout my years of high school, I played my trumpet, swung my bat, took pictures for the yearbook, wrote a weekly article for the local newspaper about school events, and even danced on stage for a drama production. All this gave me the confidence to then try out for cheerleading as well as become an officer for my band and the honor society; then, one day. . . . I realized I had crossed the line into another space in which the word *acceptance* took on meaning beyond me.

One evening of my senior year, I was studying at home when I got a call. Several of my classmates who I had come to know over my high school years in our college track classes called me at home to tell me,

"You made Top Ten!"

Our high school had, and continues to have, a strong Homecoming tradition. During my high school years, a list containing the senior girls' names would be distributed to the entire student body who would vote for ten girls from the list. The ten who receive the most votes become what are known as "Top Ten." My unexpected call led me to jump in my car and verify that what these girls were telling me was actually true. I drove the few miles down the road to the high school with the sun setting to the west behind Mt. Diablo. A small crowd of students just getting out of football practice and other fall sports had assembled outside the posting. They made way as I walked up to the list and, sure enough, my name, along with nine others was circled.

Within a week, after newspaper coverage on the announcement of the Ten and a ripple of excitement throughout the Student Body about whom "made it" and who students wanted to elect for their Homecoming Queen, the senior class and football team voted for five from the ten. Again, a call in the evening, name circled on a posting. Next, the student body would receive a list that, this time, held only the names of the five. Each member of the student body would cast their vote for one.

Traditions have purpose; they bring people together through common rituals and promote values that bind people within a delineated social space. Our family had traditions such as making tamales together during the holidays or participating in the traditions that our religion celebrated. These were traditions relegated to family or church. Exposure to traditions from the larger community was experienced only by contact in shared spaces. While traditions help define our reality and bring people closer to one another through the symbolism of socially sanctioned events, the degree of participation by all people in a community varies with the extent by which people feel included. Being placed in the center of such a tradition, without my consent or permission, created an experience that changed and challenged the very nature of how the tradition of Homecoming was perceived and to whom this tradition belonged.

I had no frame of reference for what was happening in preparation for the Homecoming rituals. I did as I was told. Along with the other four candidates, we showed up on time for formal yearbook photo sessions, were interviewed by the local newspaper for a big spread complete with pictures, acquired formal gowns for the parade and knee-length dresses for the rally. Then, we each selected two young men to escort us into the Homecoming Rally to which families were invited and where the formal announcement for Homecoming Queen would be made.

Homecoming in small towns can be electrifying. At least, this is what I remember. The vibrancy and pageantry of this particular rally were magnified by having the event in a small gym that held 1,000-plus people.

The bleachers were filled with confetti throwing students. My mother sat in the front row of a block of folding chairs arranged on the gym floor to accommodate guests. She was designated to represent our family as my father's shift at the steel mill wouldn't be over in time for him to attend. My brother was also working. The band and football team occupied seating also on the floor, with a row of empty seats placed in front of the football team where the five candidates would soon be seated.

The Homecoming Rally opened with the band playing the school song. Cheerleaders led each class in spirited chants to see which class yelled the loudest for the privilege of earning the "Spirit Jug." Despite the fact that the students' daily experience consisted of separate spaces in which differentiated academic preparation resulted in different outcomes, this was the shared space in which collective voices joined for a common purpose. Subsequently, the amount of confetti thrown into the air made it nearly impossible to distinguish faces in the stands. The volume from the yelling and noisemakers that accentuated the end of each cheer was deafening.

Then, each of the final five candidates for Homecoming Queen was introduced, one by one. Linked, arm in arm, with two members of the football team, we were each escorted to one of the empty chairs where we watched further class competitions, heard speeches from the team captains, and laughed at hilarious skits. The rally came to a close when it was time for the announcement to be made.

The school principal stepped up to the microphone. As if on cue, the entire student body, faculty, and guests fell eerily silent. He opened an envelope, pulled out a piece of paper, and said, "The 1976 Homecoming Queen is . . ."

He said my name . . . and suddenly things were not normal anymore.

I was rushed by students who charged down from the stands. The last image I had before being pommeled by the stream of people that were knocking me backward while still sitting in my folding chair was of my mother. At the moment she heard my name her mouth dropped open and her hands clutched her face. The announcement was timed only minutes before the bell marked the end of the school day but, after managing to stand up, I was able to receive the hugs and congratulations of those who stayed long after the bell. After the crowd dissipated, it was time to prepare for the evening's events. The rest of the afternoon and evening, went, I am sure, just as it had for every other young woman who had had her name announced for this event in the previous 75 years of the school's history. . . if they had Homecomings going back to 1902. And for me, the honor bestowed meant nothing less.

A girlfriend, Diane, drove me home from the Rally in her open air jeep. We honked and waved at everyone the distance from the parking lot to my home, the sun still shining above Mount Diablo yet to make it's early fall season descent. My mother, who had gone directly home after the announcement, greeted me at the door. No longer holding a look of shock on her face I had not considered, at the time, what this meant for her and that perhaps it meant even more than it did for me. At the Rally, she had been sitting next to the mother of one of the other candidates. She knew this other parent because my parents, brother, and I had worked for this woman's family farm in their fields and packing sheds. The expression on the face of that parent at the moment of the announcement was a sharp contrast to that on my mother's. Yet, at the time, I failed to understand the significance which is why I was dumbfounded over what happened when I got home. She told me to take a nap. Despite my wildly beating heart that urged me to bounce off the walls, I respectfully obliged her, laid down, and stared at the ceiling until she felt I had "rested" enough for the evening's events. The whole time I lay on the bed with heart racing, she sat quietly in the room, facing me, rocking back and forth in her chair. She said nothing but vigilantly watching me during my feigned "nap."

I was allowed to get up from my "nap" when another girlfriend, Debbie, arrived at my home. Debbie helped me put on my makeup, and fix my hair for the parade and Homecoming game. I put on my formal gown and returned to town. A chauffeured convertible took me through the streets of the town during the parade where throngs of people lined the route as they watched from the sidewalk. The parade ended at the football field where the Homecoming court was then seated on the sidelines of the game where at half time, the formal coronation took place. All of it was special. All of it is memorable. Not a moment would be different if I could make it so despite the fact that I failed to understand the significance of new ground being broken. I did not comprehend that the announcement of being voted for this honor by a predominantly Euro-American student body,

Was not normal.

The energy around me on campus was different after that. There were those from the student body who had given me their vote. Then, there was a polarizing and oppositional force that scowled at the announcement of my name. I am not referring to those, necessarily, who voted for one of the other four candidates to win this coveted title but rather, those students and adults who, at a visceral level, could not accept my being their school's Homecoming Queen.

Those on the extreme end of disapproval made themselves known. I was told by one individual, Euro-American, that the only reason I had won was because, "... all the Mexicans" had voted for me. I found this statement intriguing because the students who had crowded around me after the announcement reflected the demographics of the school population, primarily, Euro-American. Nonetheless, I would have been happy to have received a collective endorsement of my Mexican American classmates but I had not heard of any open campaigning from them on my behalf. Then, several senior girls announced to me that they were going to propose that another Homecoming be created for the basketball season. They would elect not only another queen but a king as well. This never came to pass. As this was my senior year, I was applying for scholarships and was soliciting letters of recommendation. I approached an adult in the community with whom I had positive rapport prior to Homecoming. I went to her home with high hope of receiving her commitment to write me a letter. She opened the door. I greeted her and though I was not invited in I explained, from her doorstep, the purpose of my visit. She slammed the door in my face. I never received an explanation for her behavior and, despite the fact that I had previously been in her home, I never returned afterward.

In the lobby of the gym were prominently displayed the portraits of each of the previous Homecoming Queens going back to times in which there were only black-and-white photos. Each portrait revealed the smiling face of a senior girl whose image was captured for the annals of school history. I presumed my picture would go up beside them but it never did. Inexplicably, the tradition ended that year. The pictures of all the previous Queens were removed as well.

Despite the violent images of racial conflict that filled the television as I was growing up, "race" never mattered to me. The fact that my mother was fair skinned and my father dark skinned had no personal meaning. I did not pick and choose my friends based on the color of their skin. My social space had expanded to include not only those who spoke Spanish but also those who learned it in their foreign language classes.

Nonetheless, my day-to-day reality would change because I had, naively, been placed in the midst of a tradition that forced the meaning of *integration* into the social sphere. Being "the first" brings new experiences for the person experiencing it and also for those observing it; their perceptions of "what is normal and agreeable" come under scrutiny. Having to navigate the aftermath without understanding "the whys" of it all was beyond my comprehension at that time. Now, as an adult, I am not shocked when there is aversion to my expressed voice and presence in spaces where my perceptions, thoughts, and presence are considered "alien." As a 17-year old, I lacked insight into people's reactions to me as social spheres were being expanded. I felt I had done nothing wrong to deserve the opposition, the scorn, but still had to live with people's sudden rejection and not let it eat at my soul because the messages were no longer subtle, they were as blatant and overt as doors being slammed in my face.

New Fronteras

College acceptance letters arrived. Sure enough, I was accepted into the University of California (UC) at Berkeley. This was my first choice. I was driven, throughout high school, to be a member of their incredible marching band. I was also accepted to the California State University (CSU) where I had been receiving, since my freshman year, an accumulated and increasing amount of funds added to my scholarship that would cover my tuition, as long as I attended this particular campus. UC Berkeley was close to home but attending the campus would require that I apply for financial aid. I had saved money since I was a child working in the fields and doing a host of summer jobs up through high school, but I did not have enough to cover tuition as well as the room and board at the UC.

I told my parents my wishes to attend college and requested their required signature for the financial aid forms. They refused to sign. Their reasoning was that I had done so well in high school, graduating top five of my class that I would surely be able to secure a local job in the community. The hopes and dreams of their generation as well as that before them had been fulfilled. My generation would not have to work in the fields. Their best vision of my future meant becoming a secretary or perhaps a beautician. Both were worthy careers where I would not "have to work in the sun."

To this day, I have tremendous respect for secretaries. If you could see the daily mess of my own hair, one would know that I have even more respect for hair stylists, but I knew that I would not be happy doing either. My parents could not understand why I should go off to college and incur debt when I could find a job that would allow me to begin supporting myself as soon as I graduated from high school.

I went back to my counselor and told her that I would not be going to UC Berkeley. The only way I could make the financing of my higher education work was to accept the scholarship to the CSU. She explained how to secure the scholarship conceding that this would be my best option at this point in life. I made arrangements to move into an off-campus dorm and at the end of summer, after graduation from high school, my brother lent me his truck and I moved myself into the dorms. My other friend, Debbie, helped me move and carried my clothes and other personal items up three flights of stairs to my dorm room.

On the day I drove off to college from home to begin my fall semester, my mother gave me a heartfelt hug, but my father would not speak to me. This was the first time I had disregarded my parents' wishes. My Grandmother Salcido, with tears in her eyes, gave me her blessings before I made the three-hour drive to what would be my home for the next four years, the view of Mt. Diablo fading in the rear view mirror.

Living in Each Other's Spaces

During my second semester of college, I stumbled into the room of my assigned Resident Advisor, Maggie. She regularly kept her door open, which was an invitation for the 20-something young women living on our wing of the three-story dorm to drop in if we desired. She was preoccupied with getting herself ready to leave for an intramural game, so was not paying close attention to my presence as I roamed around her dorm room chatting about insignificant events of the day. I stumbled upon a box of cards situated on her bed stand. These were the cards that the dorm residents completed prior to our move to the dorm. The cards contained information pertaining to our major, our hobbies, music we liked, etc. . . . that enabled the Resident Advisors to match us with compatible roommates.

I was browsing through the cards to see what my other dorm mates had written. I knew each and every one of them, some more than others as I had spent long hours studying with some and partying with others. I had the impression that the other young women from my wing had relatively good relationships with one another as it was not uncommon for us to stroll down to the dining commons together and share a meal or crash in on one another's rooms for a long evening of aimless conversation. The information I saw on the cards of these now familiar dorm mates did not surprise me at all. By then, I knew the declared majors of each of my dorm mates, the type of music they liked, and even their study (or lack of) habits. All of the information I read was predictable until I came upon one card which I pulled out and held close to my face to ensure that I was correctly reading what was being conveyed.

The card belonged to a dorm mate, Gail, who lived in the suite directly across the hall from my room. I stopped Maggie from her frenzied search for her soccer cleats and handed her the card. She silently read the words on the 5 by 8 card. Within moments, the flush of her face revealed the discomfort caused by the content inscribed by the Euro-American dorm mate who lived on my wing. The card requested,

"No minority roommates."

Maggie turned from the card and, with downcast eyes saw the hurt and anger in mine. She put the card back in the box and quickly turned away not knowing what to say. I filled the silence,

"How can this be, Maggie? We are past the Civil Rights Era. People aren't supposed to think this way."

Maggie fumbled for the right words but could not conjure up a response to the situation. She had been trained in conflict resolution, CPR, First Aid, and knew what to do in an emergency should one of her charges encounter a severe situation, but did not know how to explain to me why there were people who did not want someone of a different skin color to share their living space. Since I was not hearing a response from her, I continued to vent my feelings,

"You know, I've been in her room lots of times. Was that not OK? She doesn't have a sign on her door saying 'Minorities Not Allowed.' Damn! I live right across the hall from her!"

Maggie searched for what to say but, still, no words came. I continued,

"And, you know she and I have partied together. What about last month? She won those two free tickets to a Charlie Daniels concert through that radio contest. Nobody would go with her and I felt bad for her. Hell, I didn't even know who Charlie Daniels was but I went with her anyway. We had a good time. What about all that? It's OK to hang out with her but not to live with her?"

At that moment while my questions still hung in the air, another young woman, Rene, stepped into Maggie's room. She had been walking by and seeing the open door decided to pop in to say hello. She overheard the end of my venting and could see that Maggie stood speechless and in a state of distress. She asked, "What are you talking about?"

I pulled the card out, once again, and said, "This! Gail wrote on her card that she didn't want to have any minority roommates!"

"I agree," she stated.

"So Rene, you agree with me that Gail has no right to believe this?"

Rene answered, "No, I agree with Gail. Minorities shouldn't even be allowed to go to college. You have no right to be here. Plus, Asians should not be allowed to drive. . ."

Rene went on a rant in which she denigrated every marginalized group under the sun. Honestly, I can't even remember the rest of what she said as I completely shut down after she made the slanderous comments about Asians. My eyes saw red and my ears stopped hearing as if a defense mechanism had instinctively clicked on.

Maggie suddenly interrupted the rant with, "That's It! OK ladies. I've got to get going."

Rene and I summarily vacated Maggie's room. We stood, momentarily, in the hallway and knowing, by this time, how we regarded the other, we went our separate ways. For the rest of the semester, I kept a cool distance between myself and Gail as well as with Rene. One lived across the hall from me and the other a few doors down the hall. I stuck with the girls who accepted me within their circles, their social as well as living spaces, and prayed that their hearts were good. Maggie and I never discussed the contents of the card. I spent the remaining three years at this University where I would graduate with my bachelor's degree. While "race" didn't matter to me, I learned that it mattered to others. I had to learn how to discern the ones who had good hearts from the ones who were raised in ignorance. Slowly, the awareness and relevance of the Civil Rights Movement began to have personal meaning.

This became my new normal.

To this day, whenever I hear Charlie Daniels' music, I think of Gail and Rene and wonder if they still believe as they did when we were undergraduates. And, I wonder if Maggie has found the words to explain the existence of ignorance and blind hatred in our midst.

2

A Mexican Nationhood Context

Mexican nationalism was expressed in family relations and everyday practices after the Spanish Colonial era, which ended with the beginning of the breakup of New Spain in 1810, and with the emergence of the Mexican nation in 1821 (Joseph & Henderson, 2002). We ask, "what were some of the cultural realities in the two nations—Mexico and the United States?" Borunda's narrative describes how her family members were positioned in Mexican and U.S. society according to the social mobility they had or had not gained throughout the Spanish Colonial era (1521–1810) and into the era of Mexican nationalism (1810–1910).

Mexican nationalism was to some degree informed by Native groups, particularly the Mexica who are often referred to as Aztecs by anthropologists. The nation of Mexico was named after the Mexica, the largest powerful Native group that was invaded and defeated by the Spanish military with the aid of the Tlaxcala Native group in 1521. The Mexican national flag represents aspects of the Mexica migration story, a migration from Aztlan (Southwest region) to the Central Valley of Mexico-Tenochtitlan (Mesoamerica region).

Like many national flags, there were many versions of the Mexican flag with variant symbols at the inception of the nation. Some argue that the Mexican flag represents the Mexica's migration from North to South; this rendition describes that they were searching for an eagle with a serpent, perched on a cactus, and that symbolized the location of their new homeland (Vigil, 2012). Yet, according to the Codex Mendoza, Mexico-Tenochtitlan was simply marked by the eagle on a cactus in the center, without the serpent in its mouth. Indigenous Elder Mama Cobb, who lives in the Sacramento Valley of California describes that the eagle symbolizes the spirit (i.e., father sky) and the serpent symbolizes the soul (i.e., mother earth); and she also clarifies that the contemporary representation of the eagle devouring the serpent on the Mexican flag today does not accurately portray the original Mexica symbols (Cobb, 2006). In terms of the flag of Mexico Tenochtitlan, Elder Mama Cobb says that there is an alignment with Mexica cultural beliefs to a certain degree. She explains that the original version of the "flag," more appropriately called in Nahuatl, a Pantli, the eagle is facing forward and its wings are spread open, and in its beak, it carries the symbol of atl-tlachionolli, the Native sign for both water and fire or "burning water."

These symbols seem like opposing representations—the fire associated with the East and the water associated with the West—yet neither one can exist without the other. They coexist, as does water when it evaporates as it encounters the heat (fire) of the sun, and it returns to its place of origin. Given that all living human beings need water and fire, these symbols were key elements to be included. In the contemporary flag, the symbols do not align with Mexica beliefs nor with that of other Native Peoples. Subsequently, the different values and interpretations between conqueror and conquered have resulted in the misrepresentation of Native Peoples' symbols. The serpent was significantly valued by Indigenous cultures, and because of this, Mexica people would not have portrayed the eagle as devouring a serpent. In Mexica culture, the serpent is viewed as sacred because it is the creature that coexists closest upon "mother earth." Historically, the serpent has been represented through the Indigenous image of Coatlicue, who represents fertility and knowledge of life, death, and rebirth or regeneration. Additionally, the eagle is understood as the creature that flies the highest and exists closest to "father sky." Essentially, the metaphorical symbol of the serpent and the eagle together can be translated to mean the place where "heaven and earth" converge.

There are other theories[1] and examples of this image that far predate Mexico-Tenochtitlan[2] as well.

While certain Native signs and symbols were incorporated to an extent into the Mexican national flag, it was the Criollos and some Mestizos of Nueva España who together led the Mexican Independence popular movement from Spain. It was members of these constituencies that gained official positions of power in Mexico post-1810. The Criollos were the children of the Spanish, and the Mestizos were the children of Spanish fathers and Indian mothers. They did not see themselves as leaving Spain, but rather they viewed themselves as the new citizens and emerging leaders of a new nation. Together, with about 50,000 Native allies, they struggled toward gaining autonomy from Spain (Meier & Ribera, 1993). New Spain had sustained the political and economic structure of Spain with the copper, gold, silver, textiles, and other significant resources that were exploited from Mesoamerica since 1521.

Criollo leaders with ideas of "Enlightenment," as had been used in the colonial United States to end England's domination, mobilized the Independence Movement from circa September 16, 1810, to the creation of the new Mexican nation in 1821 (Vigil, 2012). Among the key leaders of the Independence Movement was Miguel Hidalgo y Costilla, a Catholic priest in the pueblo of Dolores in the state of Guanajuato. In this place and moment in time, Hidalgo gave the "Grito de Dolores" or the call for independence when he was discovered as conspiring to form the Independence Movement. Hidalgo had an extensive sociopolitical network that included a number of Native communities, Criollo military generals, wealthy Criollo women involved in charity, Mestizo prisoners, and the general public that he encountered in his everyday role as a religious leader. Certain leaders of note include Religious Leader Jose Maria Morelos y Pavon, Military General Ignacio Jose de Allende, and Josefa Otriz de Dominguez. These agents of social change among others and various constituencies in the Movement, including the prisoners that Hidalgo released right before the Grito de Dolores, were instrumental in the breakup of New Spain—starting with the cities of Celaya, Queretaro, Guanajuato, Mexico City, and then the whole nation.

---

[1] For example, in the Caxcan and Huichol cultures, the serpent represents the serpent clouds (or Mixcoatl) and the eagle represents the sun. It is the sun devouring the clouds; in this sense, Mexica art and language were metaphorical and not literal (Luna, 2012; Marcos, 2006).

[2] The image of the Mexica's Quetzalcoatl and also the Mayan's Kukulkan represent the joining of sky, earth, and water with the artistic rendering of a feathered serpent.

With a spirit of social movement spreading to various cities and pueblos, Hidalgo sanctioned a flag for the Independence Movement with the symbol of the Virgin de Guadalupe, which became the banner for Mexican nationalism. Since 1521, the sign of the Virgin de Guadalupe signified the ideas of "hope and unity," "long live the people," and "end oppression." Yet for many, the Independence won from Spain came to mean that Criollos would replace the Spanish elite in official positions of leadership, who then struggled for federalist and centralist political power in Mexico for many years to come. The ongoing struggle for power was reflected in the fact that in the years "between 1824 and 1835 there were sixteen changes in the presidency of Mexico" (Meier & Ribera, 1993, p. 53). In many ways, the high political turnover in leadership and the instability of political parties, as well as the rapid Anglo American migration with the ideology of Manifest Destiny into the Northern regions of Mexico all together created the conditions that enabled the United States to invade, declare war, and annex Mexican states. It started with Texas in 1845, followed by Nuevo Mexico, Sonora, and Alta California.

U.S. military forces marched into central Mexico and reached Mexico City by 1847. They occupied the Mexican capital until the Treaty of Guadalupe Hidalgo was signed.[3] In theory, the Treaty of Guadalupe Hidalgo promised that the estimated 80,000 Mexicans residing in the U.S. Southwest would acquire U.S. citizenship and maintain property (Meier & Ribera, 1993). In practice, it was mainly Spanish–Mexicans, and not the large numbers of Mestizo-Mexicans or Indian–Mexicans, who acquired civil and political rights (Menchaca, 1995). The United States acquired what became the states of Arizona, California, Nevada, New Mexico, Utah, and half of Colorado. This completed the Westward Expansion project as well as created the Gold Rush economy. The invaders did not express much interest in acquiring the entire nation of Mexico because some of the U.S. Southern political elites did not want to manage lands occupied by a majority Mestizo and Indian population which did not conform to their racial purity or would not uphold the ideology of White Supremacy (Almaguer, 1994). Yet, the United States was very interested in maintaining a political economic relationship with Mexico, especially during the industrialization era in the 1900s.

By 1910, the United States became one of the major foreign investors in Mexico, enabled through the encouragement of Mexican Dictator

---

[3] The Treaty of Guadalupe Hidalgo was brought by Nicholas Trist to Mexico, and it was signed by Mexican President Peña de la Peña and by U.S. President James K. Polk.

President Porfirio Diaz (Barry, 1995; Meier & Ribera, 1993).[4] The era of the Diaz presidency became known as the period during which the United States was allowed to take advantage of railroad subsidies as well as mineral and oil development, and especially Diaz's liberal land policy. The railroad was used primarily for the export of valuable Indigenous minerals and resources. Meier and Ribera (1993) state that, "by the beginning of the twentieth century, as European and American businessmen extended their influence, Mexico had become known as the mother of foreigners and the stepmother of Mexicans" (p. 104).

The economic gap increased between the large number of landless peasants and the few landowners who directly benefited from the array of policies during this period. Vigil (2012) describes that, "the hacendados [landowners], comprising approximately one thousand families, controlled 90 percent of the land, while 85 percent of the rural population was landless" (p. 191). According to Meier and Ribera, "Additional property became available to large landowners, mostly foreign speculators, and the result of legislation such as the Lay Lerdo (the Lerdo Law 1856) which brought about the breakup and sale of Indian communal lands" (Meier & Ribera, 1993, p. 104). In other words, this period heavily dispossessed Natives from their lands and granted foreigners access to their land. Also, under the Diaz government, Mexican officials worked with "positivist ideas" toward "progress." Like the United States, the Mexican government drew upon biological and cultural theories to rationalize how Indigenous racial ethnic members of society were deemed inferior and how non-Indigenous were granted a place in society. Many Mexican officials believed that "Indians" and their culture were "inferior" and therefore set out to Europeanize Mexico's Indians (Meier & Ribera, 1993; Urrieta, 2003). These conditions, including Native resistance, and the high mortality rate in rural Mexico, compelled social unrest in the nation and created both internal and external migration patterns to the United States.

The year 1910 marked the beginning of the Mexican Revolution with men and women calling for *"tierra y libertad"* (land and liberty), which lasted until 1920. Diaz[5] was forced to resign in 1911 and he was replaced by Francisco I. Madero. Famous rebels like Pancho Villa from the North of Mexico and Emiliano Zapata from the South of Mexico, both of whom

---

[4] Diaz came into power in 1876 and stayed until he was removed in 1910 because of his dictatorship style of leadership in Mexico. He had served in the successful Mexican war against the French, on May 5, 1862 (Cinco de Mayo), in Puebla, Mexico, but later broke with his commander-in-chief, Benito Juarez, to later run against him in the presidential elections (Meier & Ribera, 1993)

[5] Mexican President Diaz, regarded as Mexico's dictator, went into exile to Europe.

initially supported Madero, were later disappointed with Madero's lack of land reform. The disappointment was also for the Soldaderas, the women fighters, nurses, and cooks for the male and female soldiers involved in the Revolution. According to Salas (1990), "as evidence indicates, these women did not always act as stoical and uncomplaining servant" of the men at war (p. 67) as they are often represented. The women were actively involved in pressing for a land reform that would allow women to be land owners as well. Since the time of Spanish colonialism, only men could serve as property owners and as the authors of history. Given the authority of males writing history, we know little about the Soldaderas like Valentina, Carmen Robles, Ana Maria Zapata, Juana Gallo, or others. Revolutionary Mexican women and men waited for the practice of land reform to occur, and when it did not take place, some formed groups of resistance while others migrated to the North.

Coincident with the start of the 1910 Mexican Revolution, the Great Mexican migration to the United States began. This mass migration took place especially in the face of the destruction of property and deaths from the Revolution, and in addition to the devaluation of the peso in the U.S.– Mexican political economy. As Anzaldúa (2007) puts it, "The devaluation of the peso and Mexico's dependency on the U.S. have brought on what the Mexicans call *la crisis. No hay trabajo.* Half of the Mexican people are unemployed" (p. 32). With the large numbers of Mexicans in exodus and abandoning Mexico due to the national structural conditions, and coupled with the changes in the U.S.–Mexico political economy that was not benefiting Mexican citizens, there came an increase in the surveillance of the U.S.–Mexico border (Johnson, 2007). This eventually led to the creation of the Border Patrol in 1924, making it harder for families to migrate back and forth as they had for centuries.

References

Almaguer, T. (1994). *Racial fault lines: The historical origins of White supremacy in California.* Berkeley, CA: University of California Press.

Anzaldúa, G. (2007). *Borderlands/la frontera: The new Mestiza* (3rd ed.). San Francisco, CA: Aunt Lute.

Barry, T. (1995). *Zapata's revenge: Free trade and the farm crisis in Mexico.* Cambridge, MA: South End Press.

Cobb, X. (2006). *Personal interview by Rose Borunda,* Sacramento, California.

Johnson, K. (2007). *Opening the floodgates: Why America needs to rethink its borders and immigration laws.* New York, NY: New York University Press.

Joseph, G. M. & Henderson, T. J. (2002). *The Mexico reader: History, culture, politics.* Durham, NC: Duke University Press.

Menchaca, M. (1995). *The Mexican outsiders: A community history of marginalization and discrimination in California.* Austin, TX: University of Texas Press.

Meier, M. S. & Ribera, F. (1993). *Mexican Americans/American Mexicans: from Conquistadores to Chicanos.* Canada: Hill and Wang.

Salas, E. (1990). *Soldaderas: In the Mexican military myth and history.* Austin, TX: University of Texas Press.

Urrieta, L., Jr. (2003). *Las identidades también lloran*/identities also cry: Exploring the human side of Latina/o Native identities. *Educational Studies*, 34(2), 147–168.

Vigil, J. D. (2012). *From Indians to Chicano: The dynamic of Mexican American culture* (3rd ed.). Long Grove, IL: Waveland Press, Inc.

NARRATIVE 2: *DIFFERENTIATED REALITIES IN MEXICO*

The two sides of my family lineage, my father's and my mother's, were rivals prior to the war that gave Mexico its independence from Spain. Yet, both sides considered Mexico their home and shared the common interest of expelling the Spaniards who had imposed tyrannical rule on the people of Nueva España. The beginning of the rebellion against the conquering nation is marked on September 16, 1810, and lasted 11 years. However, when the final Spanish viceroy, officer, and soldier were expelled in 1821, both sides of my family were still left standing on opposite sides of the social spectrum.

In some ways, freedom was gained for the people of Mexico but the freedom was limited to that from a conquering nation. What persisted past 1821, however, were deep inequities between the wealthy criollos, my mother's side of the family, and the Native people of my father's family. The parallel realities between these two sides of the family persisted despite their relationship to the new republic of Mexico. So, while it was true that Spain no longer held the same chokehold on the people and resources of Mexico (including Alta California) as they had since 1519, the meaning of what it meant to be "Mexican" in this new nation called "Mexico" was defined by variance in privileges and statuses that endured throughout the Mexican National era. This disparity persists to present day and explains why my father's side of the family was direly tenacious in leaving their homeland despite the unwelcoming manner in which they were received in the United States.

My father, Henry Martinez, Sr., first crossed the line in the sand, the U.S.–Mexican border, with his parents when he was four years old. He was the youngest child of five sons and four daughters born to José and Guadalupe Martinez. I called them Papa José and Mama Lupe. They were descendants of the Purépecha Nation who, according to oral tradition, have origins that trace back to what is now called the Four Corners region of the United States. The migration of the Purépecha people to the Valley of Mexico occurred several thousand years ago. Their southward migration must have taken hundreds of years before they settled in what is now called the States of Michoacán and Guanajuato, Mexico. These regions of Mexico are well-known for where the spirit of war kick-started the uprising against the Spaniards, or, as they were referred to many years ago, los *gachuipines*.

After ousting this foreign intruder in 1821, the people of the newly found nation of Mexico were left beleaguered. Three hundred years of foreign occupation and imposition would tax even the strongest of heart. Yet, there were still foreign powers that wanted what could be gained from the resources that existed from the earth and from the bodies of those who were already here. Subsequently, despite expelling Spaniards' multi-century hold, the revolt against Spain marked only the beginning of a series of repeated efforts by people of the Americas to rid themselves of the yoke of alien control. What followed, despite being depleted from this extended occupation were ongoing defensive efforts to resist aggressive invasions provoked by the United States, in 1846, and then the French, in 1862.

The Mexican people threw, literally, what they could at these invading forces but not much was left. The United States, as spoils of war, claimed a major part of Mexico's territory. It pushed as many Mexicans as possible to the other side of a new line, also known as "the border," drawn in the sand. Guanajuato was already on "that side" (Mexico) so at least the Martinez family, my father's side of the family, did not have to deal with another invader claiming and then squatting on their ancestral lands. They were still left to deal, however, with the invaders who followed and profited in the wake of Cortés' military victories. The presence of these benefactors still had an adverse effect. This would be, for example, my mother's side of the family, the Garcias, who had settled in the State of Chihuahua. So, after the last pistol had fired in celebration of Mexican independence from Spain, all the dancing had ended, and the dust settled, the Martinez family found itself in circumstances not much different from before the fight for freedom from Spain. They adapted to this new reality, for a short while, but eventually their self-determination fueled their quest to live beyond the yoke of generational and systemic colonization.

Life Above the Line Drawn in the Sand

Whether a person with Native ancestry ended up south or north of the border, the treatment was the same; aggression marked one's reality. Those who had to sustain invasion of their ancestral homelands by the Spaniards who came from the South or by the U.S. Americans who crossed plains and climbed mountains from the East battled every form of aggressive weapon of genocide from divide and conquer, to germs and weapons. When even these forces were unable to eradicate surviving numbers of Native humanity, relocation to reservations which were often the least desirable land became an additional weapon by which to "control" Native people.

After a considerable portion of Mexican territory was lost to the United States, the people who had received and profited from Spanish land grants were now considered aliens and foreigners on the very land they considered their home. Anyone, north of the border, who spoke Spanish was marked for expulsion. The enmity between the remaining Spanish criollos still living in Alta California during the Mexican era and the westward seeking Europeans searching for gold, and then desiring land, set the stage for numerous skirmishes and massacres. Despite the fact that an article in the treaty between Mexico and the United States protected the rights of Mexicans to their property in California, the discovery of gold brought encroachment, displacement, and embitterment to the people whose deeds to land were disregarded. Their cattle was parceled out and slaughtered by encroachers.

Growing enmity between Mexicans (formerly criollos and also Mestizos) and expansionists as well as gold seekers fueled the reputation, fear, and legend of Joaquin Murieta who sought legal response for the violation committed on his wife. Legal authorities refused to seek justice for the crime committed and after the offenders discovered that Murieta had sought legal intervention, they publicly whipped him. His wife, being provided an account of his whipping, mistakenly believed he was dead and subsequently took her own life. After Murieta recovered from the brutal attack he vindicated his wife's honor as well as his own. He sought out and killed each and every one of the men who had violated his wife and who had participated in his public humiliation.

The turbulence on both sides of the U.S.–Mexican border during this era is replete with examples of oppositional forces speaking to one another through the barrels of their guns. On the north side of the border, the threat induced by the growing legend of Joaquin Murieta hung in the air. So, when a group of approximately 12 men, mostly Spanish-speaking, committed what is famously known in the Gold Country as the Rancheria Murder of 1855 in which six white men, one woman, and an Indian were killed, the call for retaliation by the townspeople of Drytown resulted in 35 Spanish-speaking men being rounded up and threatened with hanging. Despite protests made by some townspeople such as William O. Clark who cautioned against vindictive violence, three men were hung to appease the crowd of 500. Arrests of anyone perceived to be a "Mexican National" were subsequently rounded up in Sonora and Gopher Flat. The vindictiveness resulted in the violent and then the systemic expulsion of hundreds of Spanish-speaking people that included mostly Mexican laborers and Chileans from the region.

In Drytown, the Catholic Church as well as the homes of families was burned to the ground. As disarmed innocent men, women, and children fled, instructions were given to those guarding them to kill as many as possible. The bodies of Spanish-speaking laborers who paid for the crimes of those who committed the Rancheria Massacre were later found in holes, shafts, or springs. Life on the north side of the border for those who spoke Spanish and particularly those of Native heritage was just as harsh as it was south of the border (Thomas and West, 1881).

Also Known As Indentured Servitude

My father and his siblings were born in Chamacuaro, Guanajuato, where all the residents of their community were related by blood, marriage, baptism, or a good story. In order to escape their impoverished conditions in Central Mexico, my father, when he was still a child, and his parents would stay with one of his older sisters who was married and had settled in Reynoso, Texas. Crossing into the United States as often as possible, his parents worked in the fields until the Border Patrol would find them "*sin papeles*" and send them back to Chamacuaro.

I never had the sense that the Martinez's disliked their home in Mexico. For example, my father recalls that in his childhood, he would play with other village children in the newly upturned soil from the construction of new irrigation canals. They would unearth old clay pots left from centuries of Native habitation and not knowing the significance of these ancient treasures they would merely toss them aside and continue digging for the sheer joy of the discovery. And, while the treasures were relics from their ancestors, the soil in which these artifacts were imbedded could not be claimed by the descendants of those who made them. Despite ousting the Spaniards and later, the French, the land no longer belonged to them.

Instability in the nation of Mexico induced the young men to secure a predictable and higher standard of existence. The chance to break the bonds of poverty on my father's side of the family came when the United States threw its proverbial hat and the lives of its men into World War II. It needed foreign labor to work its unattended crops, so with carefully constructed stipulations by which to meet its needs, the United States placed a call to its southern neighbor. Subsequently, people from "South of the Border," who were previously rounded up and dumped on the other side for working "undocumented" in the United States, were then provided "conditional employment" for entry to the country. My father's older brothers heeded the call. They traveled by train throughout the United States, worked the fields, and earned money that was sent back home to sustain the family in

Guanajuato. This contractual arrangement between the United States and Mexico was called the "Bracero Program," another name for indentured servitude.

During the winter season when there were no longer crops to tend in the United States, the Martinez brothers returned to their village of Chamacuaro. Huddled around the hearth of the family fire, they regaled the family with tales of cities where the flip of a switch made a room light up and water poured out of faucets rather than drawn with buckets from the river. They excited the senses with tales from a land referred to as "El Norte." Henry, my father, was not one to be left behind. He lied about his age so he could join his older brothers on the next northbound journey. He rode the train cars with his older brothers on the migrant farm worker trail that took them to faraway cities that still bore the names given by the people who first lived on the lands. Chicago and Seattle were but a few of the cities bearing indigenous names.

World War II only lasted so long. Once the soldiers came home, the need for hired hands came into question. By 1964, after diminishing need and decreased regulation of the program that opened the door for greater worker abuse and exploitation, the entire program came to a screeching halt. Nonetheless, conditions in Mexico had not improved; peace between the haves and the have-nots was yet to be a reality.

The incentives to return to the United States were greater than the reasons not to.

The oldest of the Martinez brothers, Rafael, paved the path for each family member who followed. He landed a job that no longer required him to follow the crops and he settled in Brentwood, a small community in the far reaches of the Bay Area, with his young wife, Regina. This is where a migrant farm worker could leave the fields if he was lucky enough to escape being crippled by the short hoe and still walk, erect, into a blue collar job in the booming steel industry. He would now have health benefits, indoor toilets, and even a pension for when he retired. Truly, "El Norte" seemed good. Life to the east of Mt. Diablo would be promising for future generations as it provided more than what the family had back home, south of the border.

My father moved to a migrant farm working camp called the Blue Goose Camp, and eventually, he and his brothers were able to secure a home for their aging parents, my Papa José and Mama Lupe. Their home was only a bike ride from the home in which I grew up and made it possible for me, once I was old enough, to ride over and enter their home through an enclosed patio. Immediately, as I walked through the door, I felt as though

I had been transported to another era. Upon entering the front door of their enclosed porch, I was greeted with ristra hanging in clusters above my head. Stepping into the kitchen, I would often be greeted by Mama Lupe who made homemade corn tortillas and taquitos right off the comal. As though anticipating my thirsty arrival, she always had a jarra of agua fresca that sat invitingly on the dining table.

In the early evening, I would sit with my Papa José and Mama Lupe under the shade of a pomegranate tree and visit; my Papa José wore his huaraches, sombrero, and simple cotton wear and my Mama Lupe donned her rebozo, loose skirts, and copper earrings. Both were the color of soft earth. Their home was central to a constellation of sons and daughters who all held jobs, got married, had children, and sent the next generation to school. Education was not a privilege accorded in their homeland because the necessity to work for the survival of the family was more imperative. In "El Norte," an education was that much more possible for the next generation when parents have jobs to provide the necessities of life.

Struggling to be Free

Papa José and Mama Lupe always exuded a state of tranquility that I failed to appreciate as a child. Their demeanor stood in sharp contrast to those of my generation who witnessed the turmoil that raged during the 1960s. I had no way of understanding the existence into which they were born that compared to the struggles of people in the United States who were, at the time, also fighting for their rights—the quest for equality and to be treated with dignity.

My Papa José and Mama Lupe were born in 1888, two generations after Mexico had gained its independence from Spain and a generation after the United States and then the French trampled through Mexico. Yet, their birth in the nation of Mexico held little promise for them though annual celebrations continued to mark the pride of their victories against Spain and France. With so many waves of expansionistic nations imposing their exploitive intentions, it was enough that they were able to secure their lives, ensure that there would be future generations through their offspring, and preserve a culture that still stands and reasserts itself north of the border.

On the tail end of a summer day, I sat on the cool grass at my grandparents' feet. They always had cuentos, fascinating tales, to share. My Papa José, with my Mama Lupe sitting in a folding chair by his side, would lean on his cane as he shifted his body toward me. This was his cue that a story was forthcoming. As my father had enforced that I speak only Spanish in the home, I had developed a level of fluency that allowed me to connect with the generations before me. For this I was grateful because on one occasion, my Papa José told the story of what happened to him when he was a young man and dating my Mama Lupe.

> "Your Mama Lupe lived in a nearby village of Acambaro, Guanajuato. In order for me to see my sweetheart, I had to travel along a river that connected the two communities. One day, star struck young man as I was, I set out to pay a visit to my girlfriend whose village was hosting a festival. *Mi 'ama* warned me not to come home late but, as young men in love do, I extended my time as long as I could to enjoy the festival and visit my *querida*."

When telling the story, my Papa José glanced at my Mama Lupe to see if the sweet term had endeared her. She pulled her reboso tighter around her shoulders as the shadows extending from the trees grew longer. She gazed off to the distance pretending to be unimpressed. My Papa José proceeded with the story. . .

> "By the time I struck out onto the path to make the trek home, the sun had started its descent. The village of Acambaro was well behind me but Chamacuaro was nowhere in sight as the diminishing rays of the sun were replaced with the light of the moon. The path along the river was narrow, wide enough for one person only. This required one to give way to the other should two come to cross on the path. I saw, up ahead, the figure of a person approaching and moving steadily toward me. Not wanting to engage whoever it was in the dusk of the evening, I propped up the collar of my jacket and lowered the brim of my hat to partially conceal my eyes."

My Papa José, one to tell a good story, threw in theatrics during this last part and acted it out by lowering his hat and popping up the collar of his shirt. He rested both hands on the top of his cane and leaned closer to me; his voice lowered as he told of what happened next,

> "The person drew closer and I attempted to not make eye contact. I continued toward my village carrying myself *muí machito* until I discovered that I would be vying for footing on the narrow path with the other person; but as it turned out, there was no need to share the path. Just as I thought that I and the other would collide on this narrow path, I discovered that this was not a person."

Papa José turned to look at Mama Lupe, leaving me hanging in suspense. She feigned disinterest but kept an ear tilted toward him as Papa José proceeded,

> "Simultaneously, I realized that I was not dealing with an earthly being as I could feel the sensation of the ghost pass through my body. *Me desmaye!* I fainted right there on the path. When I came to, I heard the wail of the ghost. This was my encounter with La Llorona. She continued down the path toward Acambaro. The hair on the back stood up and I ran as fast as I could the rest of the way to my village. From that point on, I heeded my mother's warning."

Chills ran up and down my spine. That evening, I made sure to jump on my bike and leave for home before the shadows grew too long.

I was awestruck by the stories shared by my Papa José and Mama Lupe. They lived, daily, with a sense of being "in time" that was for me, as a child, an experiential reality that I learned to appreciate. It was not until I was an adult, however, that I came to understand how they came to live and cherish each moment; because it was not always this way for them. Generations before Papa José and Mama Lupe and even in their own early lives, they did not work for themselves, did not own their time, or even own themselves; they were relegated to enslavement on the land of their ancestors in a system much akin to the Southern Plantations of the United States in which people were held bound, dependent, and against their will. They had been subjected to work under forced labor and varied forms and degrees of mistreatment.

A Veiled System of Slavery

Chamacuaro, Guanajuato, was home to my father's side of the family for centuries since their migration to the Valley of Mexico from the Four Corners region of the United States. After the first Spaniard on horseback arrived, the Purépecha continued to live on the land, but the land was soon to be claimed by those who came on horseback. The land on which my grandparents and their ancestors lived was no longer *theirs*. This did not transpire so easily. Many bitter battles raged between the Purépecha and the Spaniards who held the advantage of horse, weapons, and disease to gain the upper hand. Subsequently, those from the Purépecha nation who were unable to flee were enslaved on their own homeland.

The Spanish Crown, intent on making itself the wealthiest nation in the world, determined that the most cost-effective way to extract the resources of the land would be by making the people who already lived on the land to *extract it for them*. Since the Spanish conquerors did not have provisions nor were they invested in raising their own crops, they created a system by which to have those already here provide their sustenance as well. In essence, they needed to force the newly conquered people to work the mines *and* tend the fields. An added twist to this system of slavery that the rulers of Spain added was to "tame" the Native people through the indoctrination of religion. The dual weapons of subjugation, church and sword, became known as the Encomienda. My Papa José was born and raised in the community founded to support the Encomienda of San Jose de Carmen.

This is where the polarities of my bloodlines are at their greatest extremes and where the contrast of the family line between the colonizer, the Garcia's, and the Martinez's, the colonized, are the most evident. One lived in the fortified walls of the hacienda and the other built the walls for them. Foreigners occupied the land, and under a system of violent enforcement, forced the colonized to work it. No matter how nicely historians try to spin it, the system of the Encomienda, similar to the Missions of California, were intended to subjugate the Native people and ensure that the people paid "tribute" to the Spanish crown.

In the early 1500s, Spanish haciendaeros took advantage of the "vacated land" when Native populations died from fever, smallpox, and other diseases that were not common in this part of the world. With widespread epidemics weakening Indian resistance, the doors for outside forces to occupy and lay claim to the land was that much easier. And, as was the case throughout the America's in which wide scale epidemics decimated whole Native communities, the same transpired in Guanajuato.

Founded on August 1, 1648, the land was "granted" by the Spanish crown to Franciscan friars with the intent of converting and pacifying the Purépecha people to Christianity. It was believed that a people subdued through religion would be much more complacent when forced to work; and, as it turns out, the land grant of two sites, one with lime and another with a quarry, were enough to attract foreign investors for centuries thereafter. Other minerals extracted from Mother Earth that were of value to the Spaniards and which our ancestry were compelled and forced to mine included silver and gold. This fed the Spanish thirst for wealth for centuries to come.

The Franciscan friars then increased the size of the Encomienda through more land grants and property purchases. They baptized this Mexican version of a U.S. Southern Plantation with the name of San José del Carmen Hacienda, in honor of his religious order. In 1664, the land was sold to a Don Nicholás Botello who expanded the land even more.

Then, when he died, his heir, who was in debt, sold it back to the monks of the convent of Salvatierra in 1729.

After the land passed through many hands, it was purchased by a wealthy Spaniard from Barcena de Cicero named Francisco de La Llamosa. This was in 1872, 16 years before the birth of my Papa José and Mama Lupe. During Llamosa's reign, 2,000 "day laborers" were put to work on the territory that was deemed the "breadbasket of Nueva España." The labor of the people who were originally from the region made considerable profit for the Spanish Adventurer and he was generous with the gains he made from the sweat and toil of my ancestors; he created a Spanish Charity, the Spanish Casino, and the Spanish Mexico Cemetery. He also channeled funds back to Spain and invested in the foundation of the Mexican Mercantile Bank, which is now the Banco Nacional de Mexico (Banamex). The wealth generated from my ancestor's labor was also funneled into the building of the chapel of the atonement in the Hispanic Westminister Cathedral, England. None of this improved the day-to-day existence of the 2,000 "day laborers."

A population census report taken in 1930, Mexico, provides context for the realities under which my Papa José and Mama Lupe were living and trying to raise their children as best they could. My father had not been born yet but seven of his older siblings were accounted for and listed under their parents whose names appear first in the column. With magnifying glass, I am able to discern the various categories that provide vital information about my father's family. Under the category of "Occupation," my Papa José and his oldest son, Rafael, who was 17 at the time, are both listed as day laborers, the primary occupation for those who are employed on this one page containing 49 total names. This connects them directly to the "labor" that made Francisco de La Llamosa materially rich.

Further examination of the 1930 Census document indicates that my Papa José and Mama Lupe are married civilly and by church. The category that asks for religion indicates that every individual on the page is Catholic, a faith imposed as a means of subjugation upon the indigenous population of Mexico and carried upward through the California Mission system as well as into Central America. One category in the Census requests whether the person can "read and write" or "just read." This category is left blank for the four aunts and uncles who were in the age range of three to seven but the three oldest indicate that they were able to do both.

Ascertaining what language(s) are spoken provided two different responses, "Castellano," (which originated in Spain and is the dominant language of that nation) and in parenthesis is the word "Spanish." There was a separate category in which people could indicate if they spoke any other languages or dialects. The entire listing from this one page of the 1930 Census of 49 people reflect "Castellano" (Spanish)-speaking only. This tells me that in a span of 400 years that the original language spoken in Guanajuato as well as their indigenous beliefs and practices had been purged, or at least not openly claimed.

One last category that reveals and underscores the conditions for my family was that pertaining to "Property Owned." Up and down the column, this category is left blank. Not one from the list of 49 names claimed property on which they lived nor could they claim any property elsewhere and inhabited by relatives. Yet, they were, nonetheless, day laborers, also known as field workers, also known as indentured servants on land owned by someone else. Put more bluntly, they were slaves.

Today, as an adult, I can gaze at the images of "Hacienda San Jose del Carmen" and it makes me physically nauseous. The massive walls, stately buildings, and multiple archways were built by my ancestors, on my father's side of the family. The grueling labor to support the interest of foreign investors during the Mexican National era came from people like my father's family who saw the haciendas from the outside of the fortified walls. On a recent visit with my parents, my father told me about the harsh realities into which my Papa José and Mama Lupe were born. He stated, "After Porfirio Diaz became President, he sold all the land to foreigners. The people who lived in the reach of the Hacienda's were owned by the Hacenderos." He stopped for a moment as he attempted to recall the word to describe what his parents were born into. I offered, "Esclavitud? Slavery?" He answered, "Yes! They were slaves. If people didn't do what they were told, they were whipped until they died. They were buried right where they died. Then, another group of people were brought in to finish the job. That's what your grandparents were born into."

It was no wonder my Grandparents, Papa José and Mama Lupe, as well as their children persisted in leaving Guanajuato numerous times despite being caught by the U.S. Immigration and returned time and time again. And yet, as my Papa José and Mama Lupe sat under the pomegranate tree with their various children and grandchildren coming to visit, I could not help but feel their yearning to be in their homeland but,

without the yoke of oppression.

So, while Mexicans in Mexico from both ends of the socioeconomic spectrum debated ownership of the land through the barrels of their rifles, my Papa José and Mama Lupe's children and grandchildren gained a foothold in a new nation founded smack dab on top of their ancestral homeland, the land from where our tribe originated and was now called the United States. My male cousins went off to fight wars across land and water under the flag of the red, white, and blue and I got picked up by a yellow school bus every morning, taken to school, and told not to speak Spanish.

My Papa José and Mama Lupe, their ancestors, and their prodigious offspring survived and persisted through numerous conflicts that would sustain (or rather obliterate) several lifetimes; these included the Mexican Independence War, U.S.–Mexican War, Mexican Revolutionary War, World War I and II, the Korean War, the Vietnam War, Desert Storm, and of course the latest, the Iraqi and Afghanistan Wars. My grandparents and their offspring have carried enough water on behalf of others to drown a whale while fighting other's wars, barely escaping with life and limb.

For this reason, I could not fault my Papa José and Mama Lupe for enjoying the evenings in their later years peacefully watching their favorite Western show, "Gunsmoke." Settled and retired in a new homeland, "El Norte," they would flick on their black-and-white television and enjoy a simple pleasure in their own way. They never did learn to speak English. Many people in this day and age would be angry to know this in a country that is "English-only" centric. Yet, since the people who worked alongside my grandparents were predominantly Spanish-speaking, and the long hours in the fields did not allow for time after work other than providing for the necessities of the family, it was the functional and necessary means by which to communicate while they toiled to survive, with the hope that the next generation would thrive. So, with the volume to their black-and-white television off, they narrated what they thought was transpiring and created their own version of the characters who postured, drew guns, and the sheriff always ended up the victor. As I think about the generations of servitude and displacement they had escaped and the relative peace in which they lived their final years, I knew that their efforts would not be in vain, their grandchildren would, as did the sheriff of Gunsmoke, prevail and enact justice.

Privilege Projected from Inside the Hacienda

On my mother's side, the connection to the Garcia family's wealth provided just enough leverage for my Grandmother Salcido, my mother's mother, to survive multiple personal losses after having to bury her father-in-law, infant child, mother, and husband between 1913 and 1918. Three of them are buried on a hillside in Morenci, Arizona. Affluence provided access to rare privilege for Grandma Salcido. Life was still, nonetheless, challenging as the dishevel that transpired in Mexico affected all classes. Yet, one of the biggest benefits afforded her when she was a child was that she didn't have to do manual labor. Instead, she was provided a formal education. It was rare for girls in the 1800s through the early 1900s to receive a formal education and those who were, generally belonged to the wealthier class. Grandma Salcido, who was born on April 3, 1895, completed her studies all the way up to eighth grade. Subsequently, despite becoming a widow, her writing skills, her fair skin, and her social status enabled her to secure a position of stature in society. She was hired as the manager of two of Nogales' most luxurious hotels.

With children in tout, she reestablished her family in the border town of Nogales, Mexico, where she would attempt to write a new chapter in her life. Subsequently, during the years in which Mexico warred with itself during the Mexican Revolution and the United States was engaged in World War I, Grandma Salcido kept a roof over her children's heads and food in their bellies. It would take more than the toss of a coin for her to commit to any other direction than where she was, so she waited to see which side of the border would best survive its perpetual conflicts. For the time being, balancing on the border between two nations would serve as a safe haven for her and her family.

When Grandma Salcido told stories that took place during the time she lived in Nogales, the feel was that of a regionalized international space as if it was its' own nation, irrespective of the United States and of Mexico. Her stories revealed a sense of not being quite there (Mexico) or here (United States), but rather somewhere in between. *Ni de aquí ni de alla.* It was so in between that it was gray.

For years until my adulthood when I heard Grandma Salcido's stories about "Morenci," I assumed that Morenci was in Mexico as was the City of Nogales of which she spoke of often, but it wasn't. Morenci is in Arizona and Nogales was a border town. Other people called it "La Frontera" but my Grandmother Salcido's relationship with that region did not recognize a "border" since she enjoyed, at that time, fluid movement, back and forth, across the border as easily as those who lived in that region for thousands of years before the national border existed.

Immigration records (Retrieved through Ancestry.com, Border Crossings: From Mexico to U.S., 1895 to 1964) tell a story of fluid and unencumbered border crossings for my fair skinned Grandma Salcido as she crossed the Mexican border into the United States multiple times. This was distinct from my father's family's experience. The following documented list of eight border crossings demonstrates the ease of coming and going for her and her children, Raul, Beatrice, Bertha, Gilbert, Rey, Palmira and my mother, Norma Lilia, also known as Lilia.

Point of Crossing	Date of Crossing	Who Accompanied	Status
Nogales	May 21, 1930	Raul	
Nogales	January 22, 1942	Lilia	
Nogales	June 4, 1945	Lilia	
Nogales	February 2, 1946	Lilia	Widow, Permanent Address: U.S.
Calexico	April 2, 1946	Lilia,	
Nogales	June 4, 1946	Palmira, Rey, & Lilia	
			1947 U.S. City Directory: Laborer
Nogales	February 2, 1948	Lilia	
Nogales	June 7, 1948	Lilia	

Nogales is where my mother, Norma Lilia, was born. Her father, a Mexican politician by the name of Cresencio Aguilera, had four children with my Grandma Salcido to add to the three from her previous marriage to Benito. Perhaps it was a protective presence of Grandma Salcido's father, Great-Grandfather Hermann who lived, from time to time, with my widowed Grandmother and her family which provided her a greater sense of safety and assurance. This enhanced freedom allowed her to maintain her independence and not have to concede to remaining with my mother's biological father. It appears that the relationship was contemptuous. No one in my Grandmother Salcido's generation or in the one after spoke of Cresencio. Whatever transpired between Grandmother Salcido and this man who is supposedly my biological grandfather on my mother's side has been lost and buried with those who knew. As in many families, there are untold secrets that are taken to the grave and the full details of this relationship being one of those proverbial "skeletons in the closet." On the other hand, Great-Grandpa Hermann was known to be a spontaneous man who would get up and leave for no reason or explanation. One day, he did just that. Without any formalities, he packed some food, saddled up and mounted his horse, and disappeared on one of his adventures, after the U.S.–Mexican war.

One evening, my Grandma Salcido's second oldest son, Gilberto, saw a straggly, hunched over old man with a long white beard on the back of a horse riding toward him from the horizon. The man looked familiar.

It was his Grandfather Hermann returning after being gone a year and a half. It took a few days of cleaning up, getting settled, and acclimating back to being home. In the evening, Gilberto, still a child at the time, would sit on Hermann's lap in front of the fire pit. He shared stories of his journey and spoke about varied terrains, and fluctuations of weather that would occur within a span of a few miles. He laid eyes on an incredible forest with huge trees that would take five men, hand in hand, to surround. He told his small grandson, *"los arboles son tan grandes que se pierden en las nubes."* (*The trees are so tall that they get lost in the clouds.*) He also spoke about beautiful white sandy beaches with a forest standing right at its edge.

Uncle Gilberto did not believe him at the time. He thought his Grandfather Hermann was crazy. Thirty to 40 years later, Gilberto read a book about the Pacific North Coast. The book spoke of the existence of huge trees with enormous trunks and of forests that came right to the edge of white sandy beaches. Gilberto was struck by the realization that his Grandfather, Hermann Salcido, had traveled up the Northern coast of California, Oregon, and possibly Washington as well. This was an era in which some people moved about freely from one nation and state to the other.

Newly created U.S.–Mexico national borders had little meaning for some Mexican people. For my father's side of the family, such freedom of movement was bound by different social, political, and economic realities. Their orientation to place and time had been informed by forces outside themselves. Their lives were defined by indications of *not being welcome or wanted* on the U.S. side of the border, and when so it was only under conditions stipulated by the United States. Despite their ancestral origins tracing back to the Four Corners region, the United States, by virtue of violent expansionism undergirded by Manifest Destiny, drew a line in the sand which my father's family was not free to cross. Nonetheless, they did so anyway. My father, born in Mexico and raised in California, and my mother, born in Nogales, Arizona, and raised in California, eventually met at the Blue Goose Camp in East Contra Costa County, a part of the extended San Francisco Bay Area. And so, *aquí estamos*, here we are and here we belong.

References

Ancestry.com. (2014, February). Sources of Border crossing data from Mexico to U.S. from 1895–1964.

Mason, J.D. (1881). *History of Amador County* (1994 Reprint). Jackson, CA: Cenotto Publications.

Population Census. (2014, February). Sources 5 of United States of Mexico in May 15, 1930.

Spanish Colonial Context

In 1521, a Mestizo lower class and racial ethnic group emerges out of the violent Spanish colonial era.[1] Mestizas/os means being of an Indian mother and Spanish father—of which most Mexicanas/os and Chicanas/os are the offspring. We ask what kinds of early domination and resistance associated with Spanish colonialism have shaped the status of Indians and Mestizos. Borunda's knowledge about her maternal and paternal families enables her to understand how Spanish colonialism shaped their distinct and disparate positions in society. This knowledge also explains the segmented opportunity structures that impacted each lineage across various eras.

One long-lasting form of domination with which Native peoples have perpetually contended is the ongoing circulation of the master narrative

---

[1] According to Vento (1994) and Luna (2012), normalizing the Euro-Spanish master narrative about discovery, conquest, and colonization of Native peoples is like constructing the Nazi version of Jewish people during Hitler's time as Universal Truth. By this, they mean that it is important to consider and even understand power relations from the position of marginalized people who have resisted forms of domination.

pertaining to the arrival of Cristoforo Colombo, otherwise known as Christopher Columbus. There are contested debates that Columbus was of Iberian Jewish Italian ancestry, but had "few qualms about living in Spain and serving its rulers" after fleeing from Italia (Gonzales, 2009, p. 13). Columbus has been represented as heroic in "discovering" Native peoples as if Indigenous people were "exotic objects" that could be revealed, rather than recognized as existing human beings with meaningful lives and societies (Acuna, 2010; Loewen, 1995; Zinn, 1980). This discourse of discovery has assumed that Columbus was the first to encounter Native peoples. However, in his research, Native Scholar Forbes (2007) found records indicating that a Native couple had ventured across the ocean to Ireland in a sea vessel before Columbus' travels to the "new world." To symbolize this encounter, there is a monument in the City of Galway, Ireland, on the shores of the River Corrib, acknowledging that Native peoples arrived there in a log boat.

"Explorers" such as Columbus and Hernán Cortés carried out the work of invasion and conquest for economic exploitation financed by the Spanish Crown. Vigil (2012) identifies four factors for the Spanish "exploration," which include (1) the Spanish centralized government encouraging Spanish nationalism and expansionism, (2) the Spanish accessing and controlling the continental gateway between the Mediterranean and the Atlantic, (3) the Spanish evangelical Catholic religious culture of Inquisition that had recently expelled the Moors, and (4) the Spanish disposition of wealth accumulation by its non-first-born men who joined the military (p. 48). The Spaniard's instruments of violent discipline and punishment, that were imposed and inflicted upon the Native Peoples, were those that had been used on the Moorish and Jewish populations in the European nations (Gonzales, 2009; Meier & Ribera, 1997; Vigil, 2012). The Spanish rulers, mercenaries, military, and religious leaders varied in their objectives. As a whole, they functioned together, and sometimes directly or indirectly as a network of foreign power intending to dominate Native people.

Native men and women resisted these various forms of Spanish domination (Castaneda, 1993). For example, Cuauhtemoc is known as the last Mexica leader who, in Mexico-Tenochtitlan, resisted the domination of the Spanish military during *La Noche Triste.* It is critical to note that Native groups did not respond to Cortés by allying themselves with other Native groups. Prior to the Spaniard's arrival, there were already Native groups in opposition to one another. This aided the Spaniards in recruiting allies to defeat the Mexica. The Tlaxcalans, one of the Native groups who had been at war with the Mexica previous to

Cortés arrival, were one of many tribes who opportunistically believed that by aiding the Spanish, they would be defeating a common foe.[2] Because the Native allies outnumbered the Spanish military, their alliance with Cortés and his army increased the likelihood of defeating the Mexica (Vigil, 2012).

The first Mexica leader to encounter Cortés and his allies was Moctezuma. There are multiple narratives surrounding the last days of his life and there is less acknowledgment of his resistance. One narrative emphasizes that Moctezuma believed Cortés to be Quetzalcoatl, the feathered serpent that some refer to as a god, and that he gifted Cortés a turquoise mosaic of a double-headed serpent. Moctezuma is described as ultimately "selling out" his people to the Spanish invaders. For these reasons, it is said that the Mexica people stoned Moctezuma to death. Another narrative describes that the Mexica people were well aware that Moctezuma experienced forms of duress while on house arrest by Cortés and that is why the Mexica aided Moctezuma in ending his life, rather than having him endure further torture. Yet, in another narrative communicated in the Codex Moctezuma, Moctezuma was not "stoned by his subjects, as various claim, but was in fact murdered by his captors, the conquistadores" (Elliott, 2009, p. 251).

According to Elder Mama Cobb, Moctezuma in protection of the Mexica sent a segment of the population, including her own ancestral family descendents, away from Mexico-Tenochtitlan into the highland of what is now called Puebla, Mexico (Cobb, 2006; Luna, 2012). They were sent before the arrival of the Spanish military and the onset of Cortés' full invasion of Mexico-Tenochtitlan. The intention of this exodus of a representational group of people was to ensure that some would be spared from the domination of the Spanish. It was hoped that they, especially the women, could safeguard the legacy and traditions of the Mexica culture. Yet, Moctezuma's controversial death discounts celebrating his efforts to save the future existence of his people, an acknowledgement that is often overlooked.

After the death of Mocteczuma and Cuitlahuac,[3] Cuauhtemoc succeeds as the Tlatoani or speaker of the Mexica. It is Cuauhtemoc[4] who becomes

---

[2] According to Berdan (2009), "Mexica rulers had a long history of military campaigns against Tlaxcala, Huexotzinco, and Cholula in the broad valley beyond the volcanoes to the east of Tenochtitlan." (p. 190).

[3] Cuitlahuac's reign was brief, following Moctezuma's death, because he died of smallpox.

[4] Today, Cuauhtemoc remains continue to be honored in Mexico in celebrations and in names of city streets.

known as the leader who fought[5] relentlessly. As revealed in some research, Cuauhtemoc is aided by a significant number of Mexica women to defeat the Spanish army, despite being tortured during *La Noche Triste* (Rodriguez & Gonzales, 2005; Salas, 1990). Today, Cuauhtemoc's remains continue to be honored in Guerrero, Mexico, and also many street names and people in Mexico are named after him—and not Moctezuma.

Native women also resisted various forms of Spanish domination. The master narrative portrays Native women solely as victims, submissive subjects, or as "malinchistas" (traitors to their people). Yet, Indigenous women have resisted and negotiated conquest to various degrees across time and space (Anzaldúa, 2007; Castillo, 1994; Chavez-Garcia, 2004; Hernandez, 2011; Lugones, 2008). For example, the Native female icon Malintzin,[6] who is popularly referred to as "La Malinche," meaning a person who betrays her people or nation, had to negotiate being in a difficult position during the Spanish invasion. Malintzin, was a Mayan slave girl, who was gifted by the Cholula Native group to Cortés. He renamed her Doña Marina and used her as one of his translators. She, alone, was casted as aiding him in the "downfall" of Mexico-Tenochtitlan in 1521. The additional malignment to her persona is exacerbated by the fact that she later gave birth to a son fathered by Cortés. Some interpretations of Malintzin portray her as the "Eve" of Mexico and that she is to blame for the defeat of Mexico-Tenonchtitlan. This simplistic idea that the downfall of Mexico was caused by one single woman only further establishes the patriarchal ideas brought by the Spanish culture (Castillo, 1994). Malintzin's child[7] became known as the first in the many generations of Mestizos—that is, persons of Spanish and Native ancestry whom many identify as Mexican people today. Without considering or knowing the power relations at hand for Malintzin or for other Native and Mestiza women, during the reign of the Spanish colonial period, claims about women's subjectivity are especially problematic (Chavez-Garcia, 2004; Perez, 1999).

Moraga (2011) has pointed out that it is important to consider women ". . . not [as] traitors but translators, women who tread dangerously among the enemy, driven by a vision of changes that may only be intuitively known" (p. 150). Different from Malintzin's story, there are counter narratives and monuments that represent other Native women like Erendira. This Native

---

[5] According to Salas (1990), "When Cuauhtemoc found that most that most of his male warriors were dead, he ordered 'all the women of the city to take up shields and swords.' He told the women to climb onto the flat roofs of the houses, where they 'scowled defiance and hatred on their invaders' and 'rained down darts and stones' on them" (p. 17).

[6] Malintzin was called Doña Marina by the Spanish.

[7] Malintzin's child was created out of the violent invasion.

woman leader led the Purépecha Native people against the Spanish military in the state of Michoacán. Other counter narratives highlight how the "Mexica women during the Conquest supplied warriors with stones and arrows, prepared slings, and strung bows" as well (Salas, 1990, p. 17).

Native populations resisted the discourses and practices of the Catholic religious institution that intended to support a systemic erasure of Native language, culture, spirituality, gender relations, and communal land system. For example, as a form of resistance, the symbol of "Coatlalopeuh," or better known as La Virgin de Guadalupe, emerged in 1531, as the first brown-skinned religious figure (Anzaldúa, 2007; Gaspar de Alba & Lopez, 2011). Prior to the symbol of La Virgin de Guadalupe, the religious figures in the Catholic institution were represented as having fair and light skin. La Virgin de Guadalupe came to signify peace and unity for some of the Native populations who had experienced intense social, cultural, political, and religious discipline and punishment in the first 10 years of the Spanish invasion. She was said to have appeared to an Indian, recent Catholic convert named Juan Diego, on the hill called El Tepeyac, the site where Coalticue or Tonantzin, "mother earth," had been honored by the Mexica. Coalticue, expressed as a serpent figure, represented fertility and knowledge of life, death, and rebirth or regeneration.

As a form of resistance, the Native population appropriated the Spanish religious institutions to some extent. For example, Chavez-Garcia (2004) found that with the emergence of the Spanish religious institutions in 1524, some Native women took their grievance of rape and sexual molestation by the Spanish military to the Spanish religious leaders. Practices of sexual violence contradicted the Christian values and beliefs intended to be constituted by the Mission system. At times, the religious leaders heard the claims, reported it to the Spanish rulers, and punished the perpetrators of sexual violence in Native communities and in the Missions. They were not always successful in stopping the violence or abuse reported. Native communities resisted sexual and other forms of violence, which often escalated the tension and bloodshed between the Spanish and Native communities (Chavez-Garcia, 2004; Heidenreich, 2007). In the wake of gender and sexual violence, intensified heterosexual paternalistic discourses and practices emerged. This led to sexual surveillance of Spanish and Mestiza females. For example, if a woman was sexually violated, or if she engaged in practices of sexuality, she was expected to demonstrate a sense of *honor y verguenza* (honor and shame) for herself and her entire family for a lifetime (Chavez-Garcia, 2004; Gutierrez, 1991). As Chavez-Garcia puts it, "Their role was to define female virtue and, if necessary, restore the honor lost to their households as the result of a wife or daughter's sexual improprieties" (p. 27).

In the Spanish colonial era, sets of relations were also largely constituted by a scale of racial and class categories of people, which included various types of racial classifications sanctioned by Spanish authorities. Among the examples of how the racial classifications were documented were the following: (1) Spaniard man and Indian woman create Mestizo, (2) Mestizo and Spanish women create Castizo (pure blood), (3) Castizo women and Spaniard men create Spaniard, (4) Spanish women and African create mulatto, (5) Spaniard and Mulatto women create Moorish, and (6) Moorish women and Spaniard create Albino (Vigil, 2012, p. 105). These racial classifications represented either a downward or an upward social status. At the top of the racial classification hierarchy were those who were constituted as light-skinned such as Spanish, Peninsulares, or Criollo, and who were also positioned in society as *gente de razon* (rational people) (Chavez-Garcia, 2004). At the bottom of the racial classification hierarchy were those who were dark-skinned such as Native, Mulatto, Moorish, African, or dark Mestizos who were all deemed as racially inferior in status. In some ways, the normalization of light skinned people may have emerged when the Catholic religious institution commissioned[8] the first painting reflecting a white skin physical image of the Christian God, represented by Michelangelo in 1505. This racial representation of god perhaps sanctioned a racial classification system that arranged particular relations of power in what was called New Spain.

Native and Mestizo communities resisted racial hierarchy, gender and sexual violence, religious conversion, and labor exploitation to various degrees (Marcos, 2006). At the same time, they had few defenses against the illnesses and diseases contracted in their various encounters with the Spaniards. They had engaged in a culture of daily ritual purification rites to the benefit of their community and individual health. These practices were prohibited by the Spaniards who exerted their power in order to force compliance with the conversion to Christianity. Unlike Native people in the Western Hemisphere, the Spanish in Europe had gone through centuries of contending with disease, and evolving their immune systems, often caused by their forms of animal domestication and population density. Resisting these multiple forms of dominations (i.e., guns, steel, diseases, and violence) was central to the continued existence of Native and Mestiza women and their communities.

---

[8] It was commissioned by Pope Julius II. For a discussion of this history, see John Herik Clarke: A Great and Mighty Walk (1996) by African–American historian, scholar, and Pan-African activist John Henrik Clarke (1915–1998).

References

Acuna, R. F. (2010). *Occupied America: A history of Chicanos* (6th ed.). New York: Pearson Longman.

Anzaldúa, G. (2007). *Borderlands/la frontera: The new Mestiza* (3rd ed.). San Francisco, CA: Aunt Lute Books.

Castaneda, A. (1993). Sexual violence in the politics and policies of conquest: Amerindian women and the Spanish conquest of Alta California. In *Building with our hands: New directions in Chicana studies*, ed. A. De la Torre and B. Pasquera, 15–33. Berkeley, CA: University of California Press.

Castillo, A. (1994). *Massacre of the dreamers: Essays on Xicanisma.* Albuquerque, NM: University of New Mexico Press.

Chavez-Garcia, M. (2004). *Negotiating conquest: Gender and power in California, 1770s to 1800s.* Tucson, AZ: The University of Arizona Press.

Cobb, X. (2006). Personal interview by Rose Borunda, Sacramento, California.

Elliott, J. H. (2009). The overthrow of Moctezuma and his empire. In *Moctezuma Aztec ruler*, ed. C. McEwan and L. L. Lujan, (pp. 218–55). London: British Museum Press.

Forbes, J. (2007). *The American discovery of Europe.* Champaign, IL: University of Illinois Press.

Gaspar de Alba, A., & Lopez, A. (2011). *Our lady of controversy: Alma Lopez's "irreverent apparition" (Chicana matters).* Austin, TX: University of Texas Press.

Gonzales, M. (2009). *Mexicanos: A history of Mexicans in the United States* (2nd ed.). Bloomington, IN: Indiana University Press.

Gutierrez, R. A. (1991). *When Jesus came, the corn mothers when away: Marriage, sexuality, and power in New Mexico, 1500–1846.* Stanford, CA: Stanford University Press.

Heidenreich, L. (2007). *This land was Mexican once: Histories of resistance from Northern California.* Austin, TX: University of Texas Press.

Hernandez, J. (2011). *Fourth world native women: Symbol for the sixth sun.* Raleigh, NC: Lulu Press.

Loewen, J. W. (1995). *Lies my teacher told me: Everything your American history textbook got wrong.* New York: Touchstone.

Lugones, M. (2008). The coloniality of gender. Worlds & knowledges otherwise. In *paper at The Center for Global Studies & the Humanities,*

Duke University webpage. Retrieved from http://www.jhfc.duke.edu/wko/wko2.2genderanddecolonial.php.(Accessed Mar 15, 2012).

Luna, J. (2012). *Danza Mexica: Native identity, spirituality, activism, and performance.* Doctoral dissertation, University of California, Davis, 2012.

Marcos, S. (2006). *Taken from the lips: Gender and eros in Mesoamerican religion.* Boston, MA: Brill.

Meier, M. S., & Ribera, F. (1997). *Mexican Americans/American Mexicans: From conquest to Chicanos.* Canada: Hill and Wang.

Moraga, C. L. (2011). *A Xicana codex of changing consciousness: Writings, 2000–2010.* Durham, NC: Duke University Press.

Perez, E. (1999). *The decolonial imaginary: Writing Chicanas into history.* Bloomington, IN: Indiana University Press.

Rodriguez, R., & Gonzales, P. (2005). *Amoxtli san ce tojuan: We are one—Nosotros somos uno.* San Fernandez, CA: Xicano Records and films.

Salas, E. (1990). *Soldaderas in the Mexican military: Myth and history.* Austin, TX: University of Texas Press.

Vento, A. C. (1994). Aztec conchero dance tradition: Historic, religious and cultural significance. *Wicazo Sa Review* 10(1): 59–64.

Vigil, J. D. (2012). *From Indians to Chicanos: The dynamics of Mexican American culture* (3rd ed.). Long Grove, IL: Waveland Press.

Zinn, H. (1980). *A people's history of the United States.* New York: Harper Perennial.

NARRATIVE 3: *VIOLENCE, LOVE, AND SPANISH COLONIALISM*

Juanita Garcia is my Grandma Salcido's mother. She is my mother's maternal Grandmother which makes her my Great-Grandmother. She was born into a wealthy criollo family who, as many generations before her since the arrival of Cortés, adopted Mexico as their homeland. More specifically, she was born in 1878 and raised in Chihuahua, one of Mexico's 31 states. After the arrival of Cortés in 1521, her ancestors followed the ocean route from Spain across the Atlantic Ocean, into the Gulf of Mexico, and accessed present day Mexico through the port city of Veracruz. After major oppositional Indian forces had been subdued, waves of wealthy, enterprising Spaniards as well as other Europeans took advantage of the newly conquered lands that were made available to them by the Spanish Crown. This Colony, before it became the Mexican Republic, was christened Nueva España.

At the time that my Spanish ancestors arrived in Chihuahua, there were at least 200 Native groups living in the region. Some of these Native groups included the Indeh, who others refer to as Apache, the Numunuh, whose name by others is Comanche, and the Varihio who also have many other names such as Guarojío. The Native response to the invasion was just as varied as the number of Native groups in existence. Some Native groups consistently and to this day resisted European subjugation while others aligned themselves with the missionaries and colonizers. Finally, there were many who were decimated by disease, exploitation, and war. Survivors of this latter group, if any, were often absorbed by larger Native groups or became indentured laborers under the new ruling class. People such as my Papa José and Mama Lupe's side of the family did whatever was needed to survive in the chaotic and conflictive reality of the Spanish Colonial era.

My Grandmother Salcido was born and raised in the City of Chihuahua, the capital city of the State of Chihuahua. One of the dominant Native groups from the Chihuahua region who persist today in the remotest mountain regions of the Sierra Madre and with whom the García family had contact was the Raramuri. This tribe is also known as the Tarahumara and is famous for their capacity to run long distances. When I was a child, my Grandmother Salcido shared with me the day she saw a man from this tribe. With a sense of awe in her voice, she recalled how he descended, on foot, from the mountain region. She was struck by his tall stature, handsome features, and indigenous attire.

This recollection between the Colonizer and the Colonized, as recalled by my Grandmother Salcido, belies the turmoil that unfolded after the first encounter between Moctezuma II and Cortés. While the native people of the Chihuahua region desired respect and protection for their traditional way of life, the invading Spaniards persisted in their quest for that which was of value to them. The discovery of silver on the land where the Concho Native groups resided and which became the state of Chihuahua attracted a flood of Spanish prospectors and Indian laborers. This resulted in the forceful burrow of numerous mines, like unnatural veins, into Mother Earth. While Spanish investors repelled the attacks of local Native groups in an effort to protect the production of mine laborers, the García family staked out a swath of land bequeathed to them by the Spanish Crown. In contrast to the western region of the state of Chihuahua, which bears cliff canyons and sierras with pine oak and cedar forested plains, and the deserts of the southern and northern extremities of the state that share a border with the United States, the García's "country estate" was situated in the central region where abundant fertile agricultural lands supported their efforts to prosper by raising cattle.

Each successive generation of my Great-Grandmother Juanita's family fought off rebellions and raids from local Native groups. The violence that raged in the hills and valleys beyond the stately hacienda walls had little bearing on the inner sanctions. Inherited wealth provided protection and ample armament within the home space where the values and culture of old Spain could be replicated to the greatest degree. The main entrance to the hacienda consisted of double-width wooden doors that welcomed selected visitors and invited guests. Heavy wrought-iron locks on the same doors also served notice to exclude unwanted elements of Nueva España's populace. When opened, the doors led visitors down a passageway, known as a *zaguán*, to a spacious courtyard in the midst of the García's hacienda whose walls reflected warm earth tones. The range of plants in the courtyard garden provided serenity and tranquility that flourished despite the continuous conflict and epidemics that claimed the lives of Spanish invaders and Native resistors. Tile floors, wood-beamed ceilings, imported European furniture, rugs, and portraits, along with the ever-present activity of *Indita* maids and servants to wait on members of the García family took on its own rhythm while the turmoil and suffering raged outside the hacienda's walls.

The ruling class to which the García family belonged accumulated vast opulence while warding off the incursions of tribal rebellions. This allowed them to safeguard their wealth for future generations. What the García family did not account for was another force just as, if not more powerful than violence, the force of love. From the paradoxical yet coexisting constructs of violence and interdependency, chaos and cultural synthesis, was born the possibility for ways of being that defied conventional customs. In opposition to the social constructions created by exerted power and subjugation, two people who lived disparate and oppositional realities, my criollo Great-Grandmother Juanita García, and my mestizo Great-Grandfather, Hermann Salcido forged an unlikely relationship that transcended racial, class, and social borders. Their love penetrated the wrought-iron doors and sentry-protected walls of the García Hacienda rendering useless the armament deployed to preserve the separation of the "haves" and "have-nots."

Parallel Realities in Post-Colonial Era

My Grandmother Salcido, my mother's mother, shared stories related to the aftermath of the Colonial era. The stories were often given to me in the quiet moments when the task of day-to-day survival no longer pressed upon her existence. My generation does not know hunger, nor do we have to worry about where we will sleep. It was the generations before me who initially paid the price of social discord and instability resulting from multiple conquests. My generation is left with the challenge of trying to make sense of the remaining pieces—our varied worldviews, different interests, and normalized systemic oppression.

A child coming into the world in the midst of chaos has no context for the why's of the wars, the protests, the injustice, the hatred. I had no conscious understanding of the incredible conflict of nations that resulted in the conception, sometimes by sexual violence and other times from free will, of a new racial ethnic group of people; a people known by names like "La Raza Nueva," "The Cosmic Race," and more so, "Mestizo." The creation of the mestizaje resulted from the merging of multiple ethnic groups of people, those who lived on this land for thousands of years and those who followed the swath of the Spanish sword after the early 1500s.

The blood of three distinct ethnic groups runs through my veins as it does in many who have roots in Aztlátan, a region now referred to as the Four Corners, and the place of origin for many people of Native heritage. Ancient migration from Aztlátan resulted in the movement of many Native groups to other regions, with one destination being Atlanahuac, the region of what is called Mexico and Central America. The two main branches of my family stem from Native and Euro-Spanish blood lines. Adding a splash of uniqueness to the mix, a trace of North African was uncovered via genetic testing that my brother, Henry Jr., had done. The paths and destinies of those who came into each other's existence in the era post-Cuauhtémoc created a set of circumstances that would inform the nature of the "relationship" between those who landed on the eastern shores of Atlanahuac, those who were already here, and those of us who evolved from the fusion of it all. The paths of parallel and differentiated realities that evolved were as unique and varied as the bloodlines of the "Raza Nueva" that were born of this era.

With the blood of both colonizer and survivor of the colonization in my veins, I, as a child, enjoyed many quiet moments with my maternal Grandmother, Ricarda Salcido, who, like my paternal grandparents, Papa José and Mama Lupe, was born at the end of the 19th century. Her birthdate was April 3rd of 1895. From my earliest memories, I remember her sage words,

No hay mejor dios que la consciencia, ni mejor ley que la razon.
(There is no better God than one's conscience; nor a better law than reason.)

I was to learn, over time, why my Grandmother Salcido had denounced the Catholicism of the Spanish crown in favor of a belief system that was inclusive of free thought and self-determination. Her observations of the use of religion to subjugate conquered people as well as to subordinate women were major factors for her disassociation. An additional factor that influenced her beliefs was her own life experiences which compelled her to have greater faith in the capacity of the individual to determine right from wrong. She modelled and promoted the use of critical thinking as an alternative to blindly following the dictates and rhetoric of institutions run and shaped by people whose intentions were often perceived by her as self-serving.

My Grandmother Salcido's memories extended to the experiences and lived realities of her parents and grandparents. This time frame encompasses the early to late 1800s and speaks of a period of time in which Mexico's region included Arizona, California, Nevada, New Mexico, Utah, and half of Colorado and Texas. The Mexican people during the period between the 1500s to the present day derive from a rich conglomeration of Native, mestizo, mulatto, and criollo cultural roots. When they collectively identified a common enemy, Spain, they rose up, together, to gain their independence against the colonizer. This mixture of people, once divided by origins and intentions, put their lives to the task and gained their independence in 1821. This *mezclada* (mixture) earned the right to proudly claim a national identity. Subsequently, the Mexican nation shook off foreign rule but its people, a mixture of multiple identities, were left to determine how to create an egalitarian society.

My Grandmother Salcido shared her recollections of what transpired during what would be considered the post-Colonial era. In retelling the experiences of my ancestors who lived in this era, she resurrected a time period through their life experiences though they had long since passed and in doing so, kept their spirits alive. In this era, the violence resulting from racial inequities raged in Mexico and was not so dissimilar to the struggles taking place during my childhood in the United States. At the time she shared these stories, it was the 1960s and I was a young child observing the social unrest taking place in the United States. The divisive construction of race in the post-Colonial era as well as during the Civil Rights era of the 1960s made marriages across the racial divide not only a cause for contention but also the target of ire from both sides. Subsequently, the response to Hermann and Juanita's marriage invoked insurmountable disdain from the García family. This direly impacted my Grandmother Salcido's life. Furthermore, despite this union between Hermann and Juanita having taken place well over 100 years ago, the scorn continues to reverberate in the existence of those of us who descend from this socially unsanctioned bond.

The recollections shared by my Grandmother Salcido encompassed the post-Spanish Colonial era while my childhood was lived during the turbulent Civil Rights era. Though separated by two generations, these parallel realities shared common roots. Our observations of these seemingly distinct realities came to bear on the quiet moments at my Grandmother's kitchen table. Augmented by the recollections of my brother, Henry Jr., who also inherited a wealth of stories from our Grandmother Salcido and our Uncle Gilbert, our mother's brother, a mosaic of life in centuries past is resurrected. The following is only one such story shared with me by my Grandmother Salcido at her kitchen table when I was a child.

Stories from Grandma's Kitchen Table

"I buried the four of them. They all died within a few years of one another."

The words ascended like the trail of steam slowly rising from the freshly poured cup of black coffee. While the steam dissipated, the words lingered and hung heavy in the air. That was when my Grandmother Salcido, my mother's mother, was left to recall the burden of events that defined her life. Deeply furrowed brows revealed the accumulation of years. It had taken what seemed like the toll of several lifetimes to arrive at these moments when she was free to give voice to burdensome memories; submerged but not forgotten.

Grandma Salcido no longer rose so early in the morning that even the sun had better places to be. She was now at liberty to quietly sit at her kitchen table and allow the memories from her past to pay a visit. I, her granddaughter of barely four years of age, was the audience to her stories. My Grandma Salcido provided my care while my parents and older brother worked in the fields on the weekends. I was still too young to join them at that time.

From the outside, the casual observer would perceive the exchange between the Elder, my Grandma Salcido, and me, the child, as calm and serene. Yet, turbulence defined my Grandmother's life and the lives of her ancestors. She bore witness to violence that was not so dissimilar to the violence occurring in the early 1960s during the Civil Rights movement, the source of violence that I observed. These two separate but yet similar eras were the source of irrepressible thoughts and violent images as we sat across the table from one another. The picture of Grandmother and Grandchild enjoying a peaceful morning breakfast spoke little to the haunting images, like uninvited spirits, that would sneak up on my Grandmother without warning. These images, in turn, conjured up for me flashes of violence and misery that resulted from oppositional forces during the Civil Rights movement. These were my only context by which to personalize and give meaning to the stories shared by my Grandmother.

The presence of the spirits at the table demand that my Grandma Salcido confront emotions that she believed subsumed in pages from her past so from there we proceed. I attempt to follow her experiences and images with that which I have witnessed in my few years of life. On this particular weekend, the spirits have forced upon her consciousness the rolling images of four makeshift coffins being pulled by horse-drawn carriage. The words that escape her lips have given life to this scene of relentless death. It is an unfolding memory she shares on this cool summer morning during my childhood.

Despite the status of having descended from a privileged family, my Grandmother Salcido's early adult life was filled with tragedy. She married young, as was the tradition in those times. She was sixteen when she married her first husband, Benito Bernal. Her life as the wife of a copper miner brought one misfortune after another. Every waking moment was a struggle even though she was madly in love with her husband.

Drawn by the promise of work in the copper mines, they moved from Chihuahua, Mexico, to Morenci, Arizona, which is in Greenlee County. At the time, this region still had semblances of what was referred to as "the wild, wild west." The memory of the Mexican flag waving over this territory was still fresh in the minds of those now residing in what was then called the "United States." It had not been that long since Geronimo and his band of Chiricahua Apaches eluded the US Cavalry by hiding in the mountainous regions of Arizona and the famous gunfight at the O.K. Corral in Arizona's Tombstone had barely marked its place in history.

Despite the turmoil and unrest, Benito and Ricarda were happy. Ricarda was the only child of the union between Hermann Salcido and Juanita García who, despite the opposition to their union, stayed true to their vows, "Until death do us part." With the man that she loved, Grandma Salcido and her husband, Benito, made the best of their circumstances. Benito made a modest salary and Grandma Salcido was a meticulous housekeeper who kept her home clean and meals ready for her hardworking husband. There were times when Benito would come home so tired and dirty that he would sleep on the floor so as not to dirty the bed. He respected his wife. A man of his character was a blessing. Life with Benito gave hope in the midst of the social, cultural, and class chaos.

As we sat at the kitchen table, my Grandma Salcido and I, she refocused her attention on me, the child, and offered,

"Would you like another glass of juice?"

I, the child, smiled and enthusiastically responded,

"I'll get it Grandma!"

"The jug is too big for you. I'll fill your glass."

With pained effort, my Grandma Salcido lifted herself from the table. Arthritis gnawed at her joints and forced an audible wince with each step. Walking was a sacrifice; each step was a reminder of long hours working, side by side, with other Mexican farm workers in the fields. Her body bore the accumulated toll of each swing of the short handle hoe, a tool that incapacitated many strong bodies. Her back and knees bore the brunt of the constant stooping and bending. On the coldest of days, the arthritis flared so bad that she could barely lift herself from bed. On this particular day, however, she was motivated by the companionship to retell the stories. So, despite the crippling pain, she was moved by the spirits of the generations before her, the spirits of her past to reconcile, in her heart, the decisions made by her own mother, Juanita García, one of the four who Grandma Salcido had to bury.

Great-Grandmother Juanita García, the Spaniard

My Grandmother Salcido refilled my glass and wondered if her own mother, Juanita, had any idea that life would turn out for her as it had. My Great-Grandmother Juanita was in line to inherit the wealth of her family in Chihuahua, Mexico. In addition to an expansive hacienda, their wealth afforded her access to an education, piano lessons, and a host of Indian maids to attend to her every need. Marrying a mestizo, a man of mixed Spanish and Indian blood, was not the expectation of upper class society. Nineteenth century Mexico did not legally bar interracial marriage but, nonetheless, it was *socially prohibited* and frowned upon by wealthy families of Spanish descent.

Young women of high social standing generally had arranged marriages. Bonds between wealthy families were strengthened by these marriages and served to expand and uphold the family's political connections and financial worth. The unions ensured that the wife and her offspring would be accorded security and heightened social status. Future generations from her lineage would inherit greater assurance of prosperity. For this reason, marriage to an Indian or mestizo, and worse yet, marriage to a poor Mestizo (or Indian) were not what the prosperous García family wanted for their daughter. Even so, girls often followed their hearts and that is what the strong willed, fair-skinned Juanita did. She fell in love with the free spirited Hermann Salcido, my Great-Grandfather, and as soon and as quickly as the "I Do's" sealed the marriage between Hermann and Juanita, the García family wrote their daughter out of the family's inheritance. An early truth revealed to me from this event in my mother's side of the family was that,

Ending the racial codes did not end racialization.

Eighty years after this breach of racial and class codes, the only offspring of this cross-racial and cross-class marriage, my Grandma Ricarda is left to reflect upon her mother's decision with a grandchild who has no understanding of how the aftermath of this marriage would reverberate for generations to come.

Great-Grandfather Hermann, the Mestizo

My brother, Henry, Jr., was given stories of our Great-Grandfather Hermann by our Uncle Gilberto Aguilera, my mother's brother. Gilbert, my mother, and two other siblings, Reynaldo and Pam, were from my Grandma Salcido's second marriage to Cresencio, after the death of her first husband, Benito. It was no wonder that Juanita would become so enraptured by a man who offered valor, self-reliance, a strong back, and the capacity to survive under the most challenging circumstances. These were assets in many circles but what he did not possess, the main reason for the García's objection to the marriage, was the lack of inherited wealth.

Why would a woman of wealth be attracted to such a man? He had desirable and marketable skills that were in high demand. In addition to the aforementioned characteristics, there was a skill he possessed that propelled him past the fortified walls of the García Hacienda and the wrought-iron double doors; he was good with a gun. This was a valued skill in Colonial Mexico where honor and justice were often determined by the swiftest and most accurate draw. Hermann had both.

Known for his excellence with weaponry, the Mexican army recruited and then contracted Great-Grandfather Hermann to teach and direct a

Marksmen School. This was after the US versus Mexico War. During his time at the School, he taught Mexican soldiers mastery of their weapons and improved their shooting ability. He did this for several years until the Mexican Government released him from service.

His skills and his reputation for use of a gun carried Great-Grandfather Salcido to his next job. He was hired by a rancher to teach his three boys the use of firearms. All was going well for Great-Grandfather Hermann during his civilian employ until the rancher's youngest son called him out and challenged him to a duel. These were the days in which men, particularly wealthy Spaniards, were expected to prove their manhood through demonstrations that may well result in death; apparently, in those days, the greater the demonstration, the greater the acclaim to manhood, regardless of the outcome.

Great-Grandfather Salcido complained to his boss, the Rancher, and explained that he had no desire to duel with his son. Knowing his own level of skill and that of his young pupil, a young man attempting to assert his "manhood," my Great-Grandfather predicted the inevitable ending of this duel. It was a no-brainer. Nonetheless, despite the delusions of a young man who was only 14 years of age, my Great-Grandfather had no inclination to cut short the life of a budding adolescent trying to prove himself more capable than an expert marksman who had trained battalions. Further lessons for me to understand was that,

> *Manhood during the Post-Cuauhtémoc era was informed by one's capacity to destroy.*

In the end, the rancher explained to my Great-Grandfather Salcido that he must accept his son's challenge and commit to the duel. Anything less would mark his son as "less a man" for being denied the right to prove his manhood; whether or not he survived the actual duel. Reluctantly obliging the request of his employer, and, more so, begrudgingly playing out the norms of patriarchal culture, my Great-Grandfather did as he was told. The two met with witnesses at hand. Great-Grandfather Salcido was not left with any other choice but to oblige and do what he knew best. He acted to preserve his own life; drew his gun, and killed his employer's youngest son.

Despite compelling my Great-Grandfather to accept the challenge, the distraught Rancher understood unwritten codes of conduct between men. He derived honor by what had transpired but, nonetheless, grieved the loss of a son. Before his grief turned to rage, the Rancher sought out my Great-Grandfather Salcido and told him, "Go to the barn and get the best horse you can find, then go to the kitchen and ask the servants to give you as much food as you can carry because if you remain here, *I will have to kill you for killing my son.*"

Once again, Great-Grandfather Salcido did as he was told. He left the ranch with the clothes on his back, the weapon he used to kill the rancher's son, the best horse he could find in the stables, and as much food as he could pack that would hold him until his next job, whenever or wherever that may be. We speculate that he eventually rode that horse to the García Hacienda where he came to meet his future wife, my Great-Grandmother Juanita.

That was the life of my Grandma Salcido's father, Hermann, during post-Colonial times. For the time being, my Grandmother returned to the kitchen table with a full glass of juice. My plate would be, once again, empty. She surmised that the child who sat, wide-eyed and attentive, would also appreciate a second helping of chorizo and eggs flanked by deep-fried pinto beans and a tortilla she called a "gordita." In my lifetime, food is plentiful.

Reverberations from the Post-Colonial Era to the Civil Rights Era

My Grandmother Salcido wondered where I put all the food I consumed. My ravenous appetite was greater than that of any grown man she had known. I absorbed the first serving so quickly that my Grandmother had yet to touch her own meal.

The few steps to the stove brought sharp throbs up the nerves of her back. The chronic pain forced her to lean on the stove as she refilled my plate. With a second round of breakfast now looking deliciously at me, my Grandmother Salcido braced herself on the table and lowered herself into the chair. Her knees resisted bending. Discernible popping marked each shift of her legs.

Through the ever-present aches, I sensed that my Grandmother considered the moments with me as precious for they were unrushed. This was a luxury in addition to the fact that she no longer had to worry about where the next meal would be coming from. During these priceless shared moments, the black coffee tasted delicious and a gentle wind flowed through the curtains of her government-subsidized duplex, bringing trails of a breeze that fell soothingly across her creased forehead. For a short time, these simple pleasures tempered the pain of so much loss.

She looked across the table at me as I would be, once again, immersed in the smells and flavors from the fresh plate of food. She noted the stark genetic differences that had entered her family lineage. These differences, a result of her mother's decision, would undeniably impact generations to come.

I rested momentarily from inhaling my meal. Almond-shaped eyes projected an inquisitiveness that enticed my Grandmother Salcido to pull down the words that still hung in the air. I asked of her,

"Who was it that you buried, Grandma?"

She took a deep sip from the still steaming coffee and then said,

"They were my family. They died within a span of just a few years."

Up until this point, at the ripe age of four, I had never encountered loss or death. My quizzical look at my Grandmother didn't prompt further elaboration. She gazed off to the distance as if envisioning a scene beyond my reach. Attempting to pull her back to the kitchen table where I sat awaiting a reply, I asked,

"Who, Grandma? Who were they that you buried?"

My Grandmother's fading eyes met the bright eyes of the child before her. A span of 70 years between the two weighs between us like centuries. I, the child, was born in the midst of the Civil Rights era, and am too young, at that time, to fully grasp the turmoil that rages in cities far away. Given this, I could only draw from that to which I had been exposed through the media and through the hushed voices of adults in my life to understand that my Grandmother's life was lived during an era in which emancipation did not necessarily mean freedom and women's access to vote did not guarantee equality.

My Grandmother Salcido reached for her coffee cup and closed her eyes as she lifted the cup to her lips and, with a slight tilt, controlled the thick, rich flavor as it slowly slid down her throat. Carefully placing the cup back on its saucer, she glanced outside the window to examine the shimmer of water drops on the leaves of various plants in her garden. She turned to me and said,

"An epidemic of typhoid fever came upon the mining town. It came as though wanting to take all the lives it could. First, it was my father-in-law, Benito's father. His coffin, as the others, was placed on the back of a carriage. The horses pulled the carriage up the hill, above town, to the cemetery. On the side of that one hill, we buried him. He was the first."

I stare, wide-eyed, at my Grandmother. I had yet to personally experience "death." This heavy word bears tremendous finality when it leaves adult lips. My limited exposure to this word is only carried into my home through our black-and-white television that sits prominently in our living room.

My Grandmother Salcido's memories span a wide berth of time that includes the tail end of the 1800s. Being only a child, my memories could only reach as far as the previous season when the leaves began their separation from branches and drifted in succession to rest on the ground. My limited recollections of what was transpiring in the world brought flashes of a man, a King, who was upset. He was highly emotional because little girls had died at church but it wasn't a fever that killed them. It was a bomb. The man, King, spoke with passion and though he was upset he attempted to use his words to convince people to be kinder to one another. My child's mind thought the King had cause to be upset. It seemed reasonable that little girls should be able to go to church and not die for being there.

I recall the somberness of the adults whenever the word "death" was spoken. Death was a powerful word that made the air stand still and seemed to foretell the darkness of the season that followed the one in which the leaves fell to the ground. Though I was still young, my Grandmother Salcido shared what life was like for her and her relations during the post-Colonial era. These family narratives were to later give me greater context by which to understand behaviors and beliefs transmitted from one generation to the next. In particular, the lessons derived from the stories about "death" taught me a few things about "life" and left me with more questions about life than I knew how to address at that time. In the end, as a child, I concluded that *it didn't matter how good you were*, because *death* would find *you*. Death could come from the end of a gun, from working in a mine, or for going to church. It seemed very apparent to me, that the 1960s did not seem very different from the 1800s. As a child I was able to conclude that,

Despite the passage of time, people still kill and die for no good reason.

The reason for the deaths of the rancher's son and my relations was yet to be fully understood. Nonetheless, there were no misgivings on my part about the fragility of life. I internalized at a very young age that life is vulnerable and everyone is susceptible to "death." My immediate inquiry following my Grandmother's story triggered a thought process as to how four little girls, just a few years older than me, could die in church. I supposed, after seeing their pictures, that they were much better behaved than me. In their pictures, they appear to be delighted to wear girlie dresses, the kind that I resisted wearing though my mother demanded so. They, on the other hand, smiled in their Sunday best, the same clothing that made me cringe and left me itchy for the rest of the day. Furthermore, while these girls apparently spent their Sundays attending school after church services, I preferred climbing trees and playing baseball with my big brother.

I ascertained that these little girls did not quarrel with their mothers like I did about having to wear uncomfortable pink dresses, ruffled polyester socks, and the little white lacey thing on the head that looks like one of my mother's doilies. And, I truly believed that while I daydreamed and pouted during the droning of mass that the little girls were surely attentive and obedient.

What I could not find was reasonable explanation for why anyone would want to cause "death." Why would a young man want to *duel* and risk "death?" What did he gain or prove by trying to kill my Great-Grandfather Salcido? The same questions pertained to the four little girls. Why would someone want to kill them? What did their *death* gain or prove? Unlike myself, these little girls, most likely, did not make their mothers mad by jumping off backyard trees which resulted in ripped stockings and grass stains on their pink dresses . . . right before departure for church.

There were many questions I could not answer at that time because I did not have sufficient information to fill in the gaps related to the word, "*death.*" First of all, I wondered if the man married to the First Lady, the son of the rancher, as well as the little girls were taken to the same hill where my Grandmother Salcido's family was buried. Then, I wondered if I could make a case to my parents for not going to church where "*death*" was more likely to come. It wasn't that I was *just* trying to get out of wearing the itchy pink dresses, but I had never heard of anyone dying while jumping out of trees or playing baseball. Surely, in the early 1960s, I would be safer in a tree.

These are all the thoughts percolating in my mind as my Grandmother sits across from me at the kitchen table. She reads the wandering expressions on my face. Once again, she is witness to my unconscious mental meandering. She attempts to reconcile the years between us and bring the storyline back to the table. After she regained her composure, she proceeded to provide further details from an era long before my time.

"After my father-in-law died, then, I lost my infant son. His coffin was so small it looked dwarfed in the wagon as he was carried up that same hill to be buried near his grandfather."

My Grandma Salcido's throat tightened at the release of the last words. The memory of the robust infant smiling up at her as he coos in the cradle of her arms caused her to pause for the moment. His name was Louis, born on the 24th of May, 1913. Insidious death claimed him quickly. He was taken from her on June 22, same year of his birth. He was not even four weeks old. That is how the epidemic was. It took the most vulnerable; the elders, the children, and the weakest. In the end, her firstborn's passing was merciful. Her first husband, Benito, and mother, Juanita, still alive and healthy at the time, helped clothe the lifeless child before placing him in a hastily made plywood box. It was all they could afford by way of a coffin.

My Grandmother Salcido recalled her attempt to bear his death with stoic strength. In the end, her heart only hardened with each cruel blow to her reality. After all these years, time did not diminish the recollection of the passing of her baby. Images of a fragile body limp in her arms were as vivid as if he were there in the moment. He was helpless against a fever that spread a pinkish rash across his delicate skin. There was no soothing his anguish and discomfort. His short life was a living hell for which he had yet to acquire words to describe. His cries gave way to lethargy, followed by unconsciousness, and then he stopped breathing altogether. The fever choked the very breath out of him.

In the end, his passing was merciful. This is how Grandma Salcido convinced herself to accept his death. She bore the pain of losing a child when she was only 18 years old; her father-in-law's passing still stinging their hearts. The blows to Grandma Salcido's reality that were yet to come would force her to draw from depths of strength that she summoned from unknown sources because in the end, as she reflects upon the decisions made by her mother, Juanita, to marry Hermann,

Epidemics do not acknowledge class boundaries but those living in impoverished conditions are at greater risk of susceptibility

Knowing she had to complete the story for me as I sat waiting patiently for the rest of the details, my Grandmother Salcido took a deep breath and sipped her coffee in a fruitless attempt to open the vocal chords clenching tight in her throat. While there was a momentary relaxing of her throat, the rest of the words of the story came forth.

"Tragedy struck too soon after losing my father-in-law and then my baby. It was just a matter of years. My mother, Juanita, died of the fever on October 7, 1917, but death did not end there. Six months later, my husband, Benito, died from the disease that men contracted from working in the mines. That was April 11, 1918."

My Grandmother wiped beads of sweat that were accumulating on her brows before proceeding with the rest of what transpired in the early years of the 1900s.

"I was left with three children to raise on my own; our second born son, Raul Bernal, was almost 5 years old; Beatrice was still a baby at the time. My mother, Juanita, got to hold Betty before she passed away from typhoid fever. Seeing life come into a world that was full of death brought happiness to her despite our circumstances. When Benito passed away, I was pregnant with Bertha. I was 23 years old. My father, Hermann, and I took Benito's body back across the border to bury him in Mexico. There were no trains or cars for transporting his body so, instead, we travelled by horse and buggy along with two young children to bury him back in Chihuahua. My father and I had both suffered tremendous losses; his wife... my mother, Juanita, and my husband, Benito. We left behind buried on the side of the hill in Morenci my Benito's father, our infant son, Louis, and my mother, Juanita. It was a difficult journey."

My legs swung under the table. I fidgeted with my fork knowing, intuitively, that the words Grandmother Salcido spoke were difficult to say but I had no context of my own by which to respond.

Hermann and Juanita's Transcendent Love

I catch my Grandma Salcido observing me from across the table. I, the child, am considered small for my age. At the time, I have dark skin and buck teeth, now corrected through orthodontic work, that protrude slightly between closed lips. My shortly cropped hair gives way to a surly cow lick. She had communicated to me the classifications of people based on race and place of birth. The "blue bloods" were those who were pure-blooded Spaniards, born in Spain. These people, she told me, were the "elite." Below this most elite status are those of mixed heritages and then those at the bottom of the social and racial order, full blooded Indians and Africans. The variances in blood lines within our own family color her world and inform our two distinct realities. My Grandma Salcido recalled a time in her life before mining camps and epidemics penetrated her world. This was when she was my age but her appearance, fair skin, light eyes, and light brown hair gained her access through the double wide doors of her grandparents' hacienda in Chihuahua. This was in the late 1890s.

Grandma Salcido occasionally accompanied her mother, Great-Grandma Juanita, on visits to the hacienda that belonged to her mother's parents. Even though the relationship between Juanita and her parents was strained as a result of her marriage to Hermann, the García's still lavished Juanita's only child, Ricarda, with sweets and coins.

It was during one of the visits to the García Hacienda that my Grandma Salcido recalls her grandparent's maids curing the meat of a freshly butchered cow. There was no refrigeration in those times, so it was a household event in which all participated in the preserving and storing of food. As a child, Grandma Salcido observed the interactions between her seemingly stern grandmother who gave assertive and firm worded commands to the dark skinned "Indita" maids. Standing on the tips of her toes, Grandma Ricarda, as a child, could see over the top of the massive kitchen table and watch the maids respond, without question, to each command of the family matriarch.

The life decisions made by Great-Grandma Juanita resulted in my Grandma Salcido's life to be deprived of the material riches. Nonetheless, when she was a young child and was sent to visit the wealthy García family, they greeted her with "abrasos y besos." Once in their home, her aunts and grandmother sat her down and fed her in a huge kitchen. They marvelled and fussed over her. Though Juanita had been excommunicated from the family, they still claimed and adored her child. When it was time for Ricarda to leave, the aunts, uncles, and grandparents filled her pockets with so much money that it fell out as she walked. Ricarda Salcido was loved by the García family. In recalling this story, her sadness came through her innocence.

In reflection of the Indian maids who worked for her grandparents, my Grandma Salcido recognized distinctive similarities in my features to the maids as I sit before her. After my Great-Grandmother Juanita had been dispossessed by her family, it was the Native people of Aztlanahuac, of post-Colonial Spain, who not only took Juanita under their collective care but who also taught her how to survive as the wife of a copper miner. Since Great-Grandma Juanita's life on the Spanish Hacienda did nothing to prepare her for the harsh conditions in the Morenci mining town, the Native and mestizo women taught her how to make tortillas, boil a pot of beans, and mend weathered and worn garments to extend their life. Above all, they taught her how to be in a world where civility was measured by one's capacity to live by the strength of community interdependence rather than drawing from the accumulation of material wealth.

Living, side by side, with women whose relations were servants to her parents, Juanita was taught how to gather and cook edible weeds growing in the hills that surrounded the mining town. These wild greens enhanced the meager meals that a miner's salary provided. She learned how to survive in harsh conditions, but, more importantly, she learned how to love fully, without condition, and how to laugh with a gusto for life that was absent in her expansive hacienda. Juanita had learned how to live in two different worlds and experience two diametrically different standards of "happiness." From this, I learned that,

Love has the power to transcend racial and class hierarchies.

My Grandmother Salcido continued, "When my mother, Juanita, died, I was by her side. She always kept a cup on a saucer by her bedside. At the moment she took her last breath, the cup shattered. There was no reason to explain this occurrence. It happened, nonetheless. She joined the others on the path up the same road to the cemetery on the side of the hill. I walked by her coffin as it was pulled by the horses, in the back of the wagon."

My Grandmother Salcido reflected on the aftermath of her mother's decision to marry a mestizo, out of love; the outcome of this decision was why she is now buried alongside the remains of those who she chose to adopt as her family, as her relations. Great-Grandmother Juanita was barely in her early forties at the time of her death. Her final resting place would be a cactus-covered hill in a segregated Mexican cemetery on the side of a hill in Morenci, Arizona.

My Grandmother Salcido finished her story of death from the post-Colonial era. She examined my state as I sat across from her with mouth agape. She wondered what decisions I would make that would determine my destiny in this restless and tumultuous nation where the conflict between those who benefitted from the conquest and colonization continued to resist the rebellion of those taken underfoot. She stirred the coffee with a battered spoon, eyed her plate that still awaited her attention, and with conviction in her tone, transmitted the adopted values of collectivism and community that had ultimately ensured survival.

"No matter how poor you may be, always keep a pot of beans and share it with those who come to your home."

I offered a genuine smile that revealed missing teeth and said,

"Yes, Grandma. I will."

A Native Context

Chicanas/os have Native ancestry and are indigenous to the Western Hemisphere. Forbes (1982) states that, "perhaps as many as 200,000,000 Americans possess some degree of native ancestry" (p. 7). We ask, "What bodies of knowledge inform Chicanas/os' sense of Native ancestry?" Identity formation for Chicanas/os, in regard to their Native heritage, is often conveyed through bodies of cultural knowledge and everyday practices (Anzaldúa, 2007). For Borunda, knowledge about her Native ancestry involved two concurrent processes. One process involved participating in Indigenous ceremonies while the other led her to confronting the master narrative as when she traveled to the River Corrib in Galway, Ireland, and discovered the truth behind the indoctrination of the Columbus story. According to Forbes (2007), Galway, Ireland was the site where an early Native couple, man and woman, arrived on a sea vessel just before 1492. Long before 1492, early Native groups had sea vessels and used them to create various connections to each other within and across regions in the Northern Hemisphere (Forbes, 2007; Rodriguez & Gonzales, 2005; Marcos, 2006; Warren, 2004). Although Native names for land, spaces, places, and people have been changed or forgotten through the process of contact, invasion, conquest, and colonization, some members of groups continue to communicate their bodies of cultural knowledge about Native connections, migrations, roles, and Indigenous understandings of the universe (Rodriguez & Gonzalez, 2005).

Native Peoples traveled on sea vessels or upon land to exchange food, materials, plants, as well as to share sociopolitical ideas (Calloway, 2012; Forbes, 2007; Vigil, 2012). Several Native groups even shared language; one of the primary languages that continues to be shared among many Southwest and Mesoamerican Native groups is referred to as Uto-Nahuatl or Uto-Aztecan. Groups sharing this language include, but are not limited to the Shoshone, Ute, Paiute, Hopi, Comanche, Yaqui, Huichol, Tarahumara, Mexica, and to others in Southern California and Central Mexico (Forbes, 1973; Luna, 2012; Rodriguez & Gonzales, 2005). According to Luna (2012), "Nahuatl belongs to Uto-Aztecan or Uto-Nahuatl family, composed of fifty-three groups" (p. 235).

In the master narrative, Native groups are often represented as living in isolated time periods and isolated places without changing the environment, as if one became extinct (or no longer living) and another emerged. Some groups not only shared bodies of knowledge but negotiated power and trade among each other for centuries (Forbes, 2007; Heidenreich, 2007; Vélez-Ibáñez, 1996). Warren (2004) states that, "Some had more obvious impact than others, but collectively, Indians created extensive networks of trails, roads, and causeways, huge ceremonial mounds, terraced fields, irrigation systems, and settlements with populations in the thousands, sometime tens of thousands" (p. 288). Today, what is referred to as El Camino Real was a Native trading route that extended from Central Mexico into parts of the Southwest. This was a valuable Native trading route that was eventually appropriated by the Spanish who later used it as route for missionary, exploration, and exploitation of both the Southwest and Mesoamerican lands (Chavez-Garcia, 2004).

Native Peoples had their own names for this continent, sacred landscapes, and places of origin (Forbes, 2007). Anahuac was one of the names used to describe the confederation of Native territories and nations spanning from what we now call the Southwestern United States all the way through Central America (Rodriguez & Gonzales, 2005). In most texts, it is commonly referred to as Mesoamerica, which translates simply into "middle America." The term America, which has been associated with Italian explorer Amerigo Vespucci, overlooks Native namings for land and space in the U.S. and the Western Hemisphere.

In pre-colonial times, geopolitical borders did not exist as they do today. Prior to contact, invasion, and conquest, Native Peoples self-identified with their cultural or geographical homeland (Forbes, 1973). In texts, various names used to identify Native groups have been ascribed or imposed by early anthropologists and members of the colonizing culture following the European invasions of the 1500s (Deyhle, 2009; Skutnabb-Kangas, 2000). Some of the Native groups included in conventional anthropological studies as connected to Anahuac (Mesoamerica) are the Olmecs, Mayas, Teotihuacanos, Huastecas, Zapotecs, Mixtecs, Otomi, Chichimecas, Taramara, Toltecas, and the Mexicas (Anzaldúa, 2007; Forbes, 1973; Gradie, 1994; Vélez-Ibáñez, 1996; Vigil, 2012). Some of these groups are associated with once occupying Aztalan or Aztlan within multiple migration times, and then moving toward the Central Valley of Mexico. Aztalan has been identified as existing in what we now call Michigan, in the Great Lakes region of North America (Calloway, 2012, p. 17) and Aztlan is in the Southwest, or Four Corners (i.e., Utah, Colorado, New Mexico, and Arizona) area. The Chichimecas,[1] as they were called by colonizers, were among the first major wave of groups from the North that had a transitory refuge in Michoacán, western Mexico, and then continued to move toward what became known as Mexico-Tenochtitlan in A.D. 1325 (Vigil 2012). The second wave of migrants to Mexico-Tenochtitlan was the Mexica (also called Aztec by anthropologists).

Today, there are contested discussions about how and why the Mexica continue to be a primary focus of Native discourses, when in fact there are hundreds of other indigenous groups that have existed and continue to exist within and across Mexico's regions. According to Luna (2010), in efforts to be inclusive, some Elders such as Mama Cobb, have broadened "the definition of Mexica to mean not only one particular 'tribal or national' affiliation, but rather to encompass all Native nations within Mexico impacted by colonialism" (p. 242). Elder Mama Cobb has translated Mexica to mean 'Mexican' or, more specifically, an Indigenous Mexican. The Mexica are often referred to as Aztecs because they are known as having migrated from Aztalan and later Aztlan (Acuna, 2007; Anzaldúa, 2007; Forbes, 1973; Luna 2012; Vigil 2012). The term Aztec emerged from anthropologists who overlooked the significance of Mexica self-identification (Maiz, 1995).

According to Olguín (2009), "From the sixteenth century onward, chroniclers, historians and archaeologists have sought to reconstruct the history of the Mexica people, who since the nineteenth century have been widely, but incorrectly, referred as the Aztecs" (p. 25). With a wealth of collective ancestral knowledge and resources from ancestral and nearby

---

[1] Chichimecas was a general name that the Nahua people used to refer to seminomadic Native people from the North. The Spanish invaders used this name as a derogatory term, meaning sons of dogs, to identify hunter-gatherer peoples of Mexico as uncivilized.

Native groups, the Mexica constructed a society with various social classes, land and educational systems, and sociocultural and spiritual practices (Vigil, 2012). As with many other Native societies that are (re)constructing their sense of past with oral traditions and mainstream documentation, there are on-going debates about how the emergence of the Mexica gained their status through various alliances, commercial as well as military relations forced upon other marginalized groups (Meier & Ribera, 1997; Vigil, 2012). Yet, the master narrative has inaccurately emphasized the idea that all Mexicans are alike and of a violent Aztec ancestry.

Although not commonly known, historical studies have revealed contested ideas about how the Mexica viewed and structured their gender roles and sexuality (Hernandez, 2011; Lugones, 2008; Marcos, 2006; Smith, 2005). Native gender roles and sexuality cannot be understood with solely European patriarchal and heteronormative lenses which often depict binary gender roles and sexual identities as one-dimensional (Lugones, 2008; Marcos, 2006; Smith, 2005). Within some Native societies, gender roles and sexual identities were understood as multiple and diverse, sometimes referred to as "Two Spirit," "Maxochitl," or "Third Gender" (Anzaldúa, 2007; Lugones, 2008; Luna, 2012; Moraga, 2011). At least eighty-eight Native groups in the Southwest and Mesoamerica had a term to recognize non-heterosexual-identified community members in positive terms. Twenty of these eighty-eight groups had a name for lesbianism, including the Mexica and Maya as well (Lugones, 2008). According to Lugones, among Native Peoples that recognized homosexuals in positive terms included groups that we today call Apache, Navajo, Winnebago, Cheyenne, Pima, Crow, Shoshoni, Paiute, Osage, Acoma, Zuni, Sioux, Pawnee, Choctaw, Creek, Seminole, Illinois, Mohave, Shasta, Aleut, Sac and Fox, Iowa, Kansas, Yuma, Aztec, Tingit, Maya, Naskapi, Ponca, Maricopa, Lamath, Quinault, Yuki, Chilula, and Kamia.

In terms of gender roles, matriarchal and matrilineal societies depicted Native ideology insofar as one traditional name and structure of family was often determined by women; and children were raised primarily with their mother's knowledge (Gutierrez, 1991; Hernandez, 2011). Among the Mexica, especially during intergroup conflict, Native women fought in defense of their families, kinship groups, and property (Salas, 1990). Mexica women had rights to inheritance and also rights to owning property. The Mexica woman also had the right to separate and divorce from her husband if she elected (Hernandez, 2011). Salas (1990) indicates that women in this society held power in that they could be strategic in sexual reproduction and gathering of food because "property in houses, goods and crops were often passed through female lines" (p. 2). For example, one area where she significantly represented leadership was in the co-directorship of the commerce related to the marketplace in Mexico-Tenochtitlan. According to Hernandez (2011), the Florentine Codex refers to many Mexica women leaders. The Spanish chronicler, Sahagún, has also noted the leadership of female Mezitliin leading the migration of the Mexica to Mexico-Tenochtitlan. Ultimately, the significance of female power is represented in some of the Native art forms, especially those existing in ceremonial sites like Tula in Mexico. *female power*

Despite subjugation, some members of groups continue to communicate their bodies of cultural knowledge about Native understandings of the universe. According to Elder Mama Cobb, the Mexica and other Native groups utilize expressions of the universe to represent or refer to the Creator of the Universe. These expressions have been misinterpreted as representing "multiple gods" (Cobb, 2006). In other words, the master narrative has sustained that idea that Native Peoples believe in multiple gods and therefore are uncivilized compared to others who believe in a single expression of a god. Elder Mama Cobb states that, in fact, Native Peoples, for the most, were monotheistic, and viewed nature as extensions of the Creator, all related and interdependent (Luna, 2012).

4 elements Artistic and spiritual expressions, such as Quetzalcoatl and Coatlicue,[2] were intended to honor the sacred elements of the Universe like earth, wind, fire, and rain. These various elements were expressed in artifacts, clay figurines, architectural monuments, codices or documents, danza (traditional cultural dances), and ceremonial sites throughout Anahuac. For example, earth is represented by Coatlicue who is often referred to as the "Great Mother Earth." She is depicted as an enormous monument in the form of a double-headed female serpent with a skirt of serpents, and a skull in the center signifying that she provided knowledge of life, death, rebirth or regeneration (Salas, 1990). In contrast, Quetzalcoatl represents wind and is often depicted as the "Quetzal Plumed Serpent." This representation is considered the knower of "agricultural education" who fled over the mountains into the South, and is associated as coincidentally returning to Anahuac during the same period that Cortes arrived.

There are many practices that honor the Universe. Unfortunately, many conventional anthropologists have repeated the testaments of conquistadores and continue to refer to the use of "human sacrifice" solely in the context of Mesoamerica. Practices of human sacrifice have existed in various cultural groups throughout history and in different parts of the world. Yet, accounts from Spaniards who came from a culture of inquisition and torture made this master narrative a prevalent and

---

[2] Elder Mama Cobb explained that "Coatli" means serpent, which is embedded in both Coatlicue and Quetzalcoatl, referring to knowledge of life.

controversial discourse associated specifically with the Mexica people and their descendants. A popular explanation to support this myth is that a diet high in maize, like in Mesoamerica, led to serotonin deficiencies and cannibalistic tendencies; but the reality has been that nixtamalized maize is high in fiber, folic acid, vitamins, and essential amino acids, and does not lead to such deficiencies (Ernandes, Cedrini, Giammanco, La, & Milazzo, 2002; Kwak, Kami, & Gepts, 2009; Wertz, 2005). Some of these myths surrounding notions of sacrifice in Mesoamerica have been addressed by Hassler (1992), who examined early Spaniard's contradictory narratives about the means and methods for practices of sacrifices. These early narratives about sacrifice mostly provide adventurer literature to a naïve readership. Hassler reveals that anthropologists have a long history of misinterpreting Native concepts. Elder Mama Cobb explains that many Native cultures understand sacrifice in relationship to the idea that human life is guided by natural cycles, in which energy flows in a circle, and in this basic process "when one receives, one gives back" (Cobb, 2006). Ensuring practices of receiving, giving, and reciprocity has taken place through everyday sacrifices in the forms of work, time, energy, sweat, prayer or meditations, and even donating blood. In this sense, there are various metaphors and interpretations of sacrifice. Interestingly, according to Luna (2012), the Nahuatl language has no word for the term or concept of sacrifice, only for *ofrenda* (offering), which raises questions about the precise meanings of Native cultural practices.

Some Native cultural practices (i.e., art, dance, food, spirituality, etc.) that existed before the pre-Cuauhtémoc era[3] continue today in transcultural ways. These practices are often referred to as syncretism or hybrid cultural forms (Anzaldúa, 2007; Luna, 2012; Vélez-Ibáñez, 1996; Vigil, 2012). Transcultural refers to a synergy or blend of cultural practices that interact and impact each other in different degrees, spaces, and places of time.[4] For example, the symbol of La Virgin de Guadalupe, also referred by some as Tonantzin, represents both a Catholic icon of Virgin Maria (often referred to as Virgin Mary) and of a Native representation of Mother Earth or Corn Mother (Anzaldúa, 2007; Castillo, 1994; Gaspar de Alba & Lopez, 2011). The symbol of Virgin de Guadalupe was first identified and

---

[3] The Pre-Cuauhtémoc era signifies the period before the resistance movement in 1521, against the Spanish military, led by the Mexica people and their leader, Cuauhtémoc, which will be discussed in a later section.

[4] The most dominant example of cross-cultural synergy is recognized through the almost universe dietary use of rice and beans. They are a perfect blend of the imported rice and Native bean, which are often eaten together with a corn tortilla that has been a significant sustenance for life in Mesoamerica.

reported by a recent Catholic convert, Juan Diego, in 1531, 10 years after Spanish colonialism, to Catholic Bishop Zaumarraga. Today, the sign of La Virgin de Guadalupe has become the most popular transcultural or hybrid symbol in Mexican and Mexican American cultures. As a result of our mis-education about Native knowledge or ways of knowing (Loewen, 1995), we tend to overlook bodies of cultural knowledge about Native group connections, migrations, roles, and understandings of the universe. Yet, as Borunda has discovered, this knowledge can be valued and reintegrated into one's daily existence.

References

Acuna, R. F. (2007). *Occupied America: A history of Chicanos* (6th ed.). New York: Pearson Longman.

Anzaldúa, G. (2007). *Borderlands/La Frontera: The new Mestiza* (3rd ed.). San Francisco, CA: Aunt Lute Books.

Calloway, C. G.(2012). *First people: A documentary survey of American Indian history*. Boston: Bedford/St. Martin's.

Castillo, A. (1994). *Massacre of the dreamers: Essays on Xicanisma*. Albuquerque, NM: University of New Mexico Press.

Chavez-Garcia, M. (2004). *Negotiating conquest: Gender and power in California, 1770s to 1800s*. Tucson, AZ: The University of Arizona Press.

Cobb, X. (2006). Personal interview by Rose Borunda, Sacramento, California.

Deyhle, D. (2009). *Reflection in place: Connected lives of Navajo women*. Tucson, AZ: University of Arizona.

Ernandes, M., Cedrini, R., Giammanco, M., La, M., & Milazzo, A. (2002). Aztec cannibalism and maize consumption: the serotonin deficiency link. *Mankind Quarterly* 43(1): 3–40. Retrieved from http://search.proquest.com/docview/222506791?accountid=39629.

Forbes, J. (1973). *Aztecas del Norte: The Chicanos from Aztlan*. Greenrich, CT: Fawcett Publications.

Forbes, J. (1982). *Native Americans of California and Nevada*. Happy Camp, California: Naturegraph Publishers, Inc.

Forbes, J. (2007). *The American discovery of Europe*. Champaign, IL: University of Illinois Press.

Gaspar de Alba, A., & A. Lopez (2011). *Our lady of controversy: Alma Lopez's "irreverent apparition" (Chicana matters)*. Austin, TX: University of Texas Press.

Gradie, C. M. (1994). Discovering the Chichimeca. *Americas (The Americas)* 51(1): 67–88.

Gutierrez, R. A. (1991). *When Jesus came, the corn mothers when away: Marriage, sexuality, and power in New Mexico, 1500–1846.* Stanford, CA: Stanford University Press.

Hassler, P. (1992). *Sacrificios humanos entre los Mexicas y otros pueblos Indios: Realidad o Fantasía?* Zurich, Suiza: Verlag Peter Lang.

Heidenreich, L. (2007). *This land was Mexican once: Histories of resistance from Northern California.* Austin, TX: University of Texas Press.

Hernandez, J. (2011). *Fourth world native women: Symbol for the sixth sun.* Raleigh, NC: Lulu Press.

Kwak, M., Kami, J. A., & Gepts, P. (2009). The putative Mesoamerican domestication center of phaseolus vulgaris is located in the Lerma-Santiago Basin of Mexico. *Crop Science* 49(2): 554–63. Retrieved fromhttp://search.proquest.com/docview/325083986?accountid=39629.

Loewen, J. W. (1995). *Lies my teacher told me: Everything your American history textbook got wrong.* New York: Touchstone.

Lugones, M. (2008). The coloniality of gender. Worlds & knowledges otherwise. In *paper at The Center for Global Studies & the Humanities,* Duke University webpage. Retrieved from http://www.jhfc.duke.edu/wko/wko2.2genderanddecolonial.php.(Accessed Mar 15, 2012).

Luna, J. (2012). *Danza Mexica: Native identity, spirituality, activism, and performance.* Doctoral dissertation, University of California, Davis, 2012.

Maiz, A. (1995). *Looking 4 Aztlan: Birthright or right 4 birth.* Northville, MI: Sundog Press.

Marcos, S. (2006). *Taken from the lips: Gender and eros in Mesoamerican religion.* Leiden, Boston, MA: Brill.

Meier, M. S., & Ribera, F. (1997). *Mexican Americans/American Mexicans: From conquest to Chicanos.* Canada: Hill and Wang.

Moraga, C. L.(2011). *A Xicana codex of changing consciousness: Writings, 2000–2010.* Durham, NC: Duke University Press.

Olguín, F. S. (2009). Family histories: The ancestors of Moctezuma II. In *Moctezuma: Aztec Ruler,* ed. C. McEwan and L. L. Lujan, (pp. 24–55). London: The British Museum Press.

Rodriguez, R., & Gonzales, P. (2005). *Amoxtli san ce tojuan: We are one—nosotros somos uno.* San Fernandez, CA: Xicano Records and films.

Salas, E. (1990). *Soldaderas in the Mexican military; Myth and history.* Austin, TX: University of Texas Press.

Skutnabb-Kangas, T. (2000). *Linguistic genocide in education or world-wide diversity and human rights.* Mahwah, NJ: Lawrence Erlbaum Associates Publishers.

Smith, A. (2005). *Conquest: Sexual violence and American Indian genocide.* Cambridge, MA: South End Press.

Vélez-Ibáñez, C. G. (1996). *Border visions: Mexican cultures of the Southwest United States.* Tucson, Arizona: The University of Arizona.

Vigil, J. D. (2012). *From Indians to Chicanos: The dynamics of Mexican American culture.* (3rd ed.). Long Grove, IL: Waveland Press.

Warren, L. S. (2004). The nature of conquest: Indians, Americans, and environmental history. In *A companion to American Indian history,* ed. P. J. Deloria and N. Salisbury, (pp. 287–306). Malden, MA: Blackwell Publishing.

Wertz, S. K. (2005). Maize: The native North American's legacy of cultural diversity and biodiversity. *Journal of Agricultural and Environmental Ethics* 18(2): 131–56.

NARRATIVE 4: REGENERATION

Every lived life is, in and of itself, a story. As human beings, we are born into a web of relationships that may consist of elders, siblings, extended family, and community who convey to us who we are. They do this by way of teaching us cultural traditions, language, values, customs, and beliefs that orient and communicate our place in the world. They also imbed within us an understanding of how we view and relate to the world around us. This is the space in which we create our story.

Within this context of observing myself in relation to the world, I came to understand that something was amiss with my lived reality. My own story was not being written entirely by me nor was the story of the lives of those around me completely under their own control. I came to the conclusion that if I wanted to write my own story, then I would have to learn to negotiate this reality under my own terms. This meant having to undergo a transformative and regenerative process; a "rebirth" of sorts of which I describe in this narrative.

We know that most pregnancies last approximately nine months. The symbolic pregnancy that led to my regeneration lasted 44 years from the day of my physical birth. I guess you can say my development was slower than most but I will account for the delay. This second and more profound delivery entailed participating in a conscious process of entering a metaphorical birth canal from which I emerged with the same "physical" self but with an awakened relationship to the world. As I have learned from Freire (1998), I would no longer be an object of but a subject in the world.

The Sweat Lodge, a Northern Native American version of a temescal, served as my birth canal. At the age of 44, I stood at the entrance of the structure in an effort to be born into a new subjective reality. Doing so meant owning Native epistemologies I had not previously encountered. Standing at the nexus of my past, my present, and an uncertain future meant owning a series of truths. The first truth that I had to encounter was that . . .

Over the course of my life I had been subjected to negative messages about myself and my people; subsequently I lived in a hostile reality.

Acknowledging the existence of an inhospitable social world was the first step in exposing a poisoned reality that impeded, rather than nurtured, my psychological and spiritual evolvement. Since childhood, I was exposed to indoctrinations that excluded my indigenous heritage. The continuous effort of having to psychologically defend and find merit for myself had become exhausting. From bearing the symbolic violence inherent in concepts such as "New World" and "Columbus Day" Celebrations to repelling overt attacks on my language, features, and skin color, the conscious acknowledgement of the prevailing hostility's existence was required. This then prompted the shift in consciousness from object to subject in which I, no one else, would construct my own identity.

Every fetus grows in a womb that contains a placenta, a source of nutrients by which the developing fetus derives sustenance through the rich blood that passes between mother and child. The composition of this organ is such that it is built to filter out contaminants. In consideration of the insidious and negative messages that had seeped into my consciousness during my first 44 years of life, I would venture to say that my proverbial placenta had been overtaxed. Subsequently, the womb in which I existed had become contaminated and uninhabitable.

Arriving to this point of understanding was not sudden and abrupt like a cesarean delivery where I was suddenly yanked into a new reality, shivering with delight at a new and enlightened state. Instead, it was a slower, drawn out, and laborious process with grades of painful contractive throbs marking and sometimes marring my development.

Toxic seepage, unfiltered and unchecked, can create a level of lethality in which psychological and spiritual distress is imminent. Any living being that attempts to survive in a hostile environment may be oblivious as to the why or the where of the sources of its contamination. Nonetheless, the brutality of each violent contraction urges a response to the hostile environment, unsacred and impure. The most extreme reaction to the toxicity is self-expulsion but lesser grades of response are evident all around.

Chronic exposure to a hostile womb can lead to symptoms such as low self-esteem, gang affiliation, misogyny, abuse of self and others, drug and alcohol abuse, extreme individualism, disrespect of elders, exploitation of people and earth, suicide, devaluing children, and inability to thrive. These are just a few of the symptoms I detected in the world around me which brought me to another truth;

I was left confused and ungrounded by the poison that had penetrated the placenta.

Each painful contraction that marred my growth and development forced me to seek sanctuary from the ongoing disaffirmations. With time, it was evident that a healthy existence would require blocking the poison. Searching for a survival tactic led me to a series of steps which started with cutting the proverbial chord from the old womb and placing me in a realm that would embrace rather than reject and nourish rather than poison.

The open flap to the temescal symbolized passage to a destination that I had yet to fully comprehend but I had full faith that it would promote my well-being. The space and place of arrival would not only affirm who I am intended to be but it would also reject the prescriptions of others, the poisonous source in the womb. This regenerative process that would be considered part of decolonization brought me to another truth,

I had to confront and refute "his" story.

For years, I had been subjected to lies, manipulations, and distortions about reality, past and present, which only fueled the growth of the malignant seed within me. The historical renditions to which I had been subjected of what had transpired *in the past* demonized and maligned my Native ancestors. These alterations impact *the present* in that this illusion-filled existence afflicts and represses the psyche of those who acknowledge and claim their Native heritage and roots. Given the presence of the distortions, a maligned future is that much more probable for those attempting to forge one's life story in the midst of such toxicity. Emancipation from this subjugation was possible in the near future only by reclaiming "our story" and by exposing, confronting, and refuting the lies. It was time to step through the open door and be reborn into a truth-filled reality.

Standing at the Juncture of Regeneration

The temescal, or Sweat Lodge, is a physical representation of Mother Earth's womb. Within the enclosure, there is spiritual, mental, and even the potential for physical healing. The word temescal is a Mexica (also known as Aztec) word in which *teme* means to bathe and *calli* means house. Those who retreat to the sanctuary provided by the temescal add value through the nourishment of companionship. All who participate are equal and join in singing and storytelling which, in turn, provides a sense of connection and collectivism, a sense of belonging. The Medicine Woman leads the ceremony while guiding and confirming us with ancient songs and expressions. Entering this symbolic womb, Mother Earth, meant embracing that which I had been conditioned to ignore and had taken for granted. It was my moment of reconciliation with She who gives life and who, without, all would cease to exist.

The temescal was constructed on the grounds of a tribal college. The women who attended the occasion of my regeneration were either faculty or friends of someone directly linked to the college which, itself, is on tribal grounds. The designated area for such ceremonies allows for privacy and respect for the continuance of traditions and rituals unimpeded. It was not until 1978, with the passage of the American Indian Religious Freedom Act that these ceremonies would be protected by federal law. Up until that point, it was illegal for the original inhabitants of the Americas to conduct their ceremonies as they had done for hundreds to thousands of years. If such ceremonies were conducted from the point of invasion, they were done so in secrecy and under great risk.

Fortunately, there were those who retained the culture and practices of our ancestors. The Medicine Woman, Regina Garcia, conducting this ceremony had gained the knowledge from others so that she, with her daughter, Angela, would preside over this rite. Our ancestors created particular protocols in preparation for such rituals. Adherence to these protocols is vital. At the age of 44, this was all new to me and though I could fluently read, write, and speak a language foreign to my ancestors, I was like a child learning to take my first awkward steps into practices once sacred to even my own tribe.

The Medicine Woman provided specific instructions so we could physically endure the ceremony. We fasted the 24 hours prior to the ceremony and hydrated with plenty of water so that the steam-infused enclosure would induce and expel the accumulated impurities from our bodies. We were also expected to adhere to the etiquette of wearing loose fitting skirts and blouses.

Our mental and spiritual preparation required that we enter the symbolic womb with good intentions in our hearts. Just the same, we were all smudged before entering the lodge. Smudging has a spiritual purpose. The smoke from the burning sage attaches itself to any negativity that burdens us and carries it to another realm to be consumed, cleansed, and regenerated. I had a truck load of accumulated negative energy from my 44 years, so was delighted to have the Medicine Woman release me from my baggage.

The water-saturated women were then instructed on how to enter the lodge. We would each crawl through the open flap into the darkness of the womb. Crawling is a sign of humility and conveys that we are all related. This added to our already humbled state since we were also told not to wear makeup or jewelry. This left us in our most natural and rarely displayed state and placed us on equal terms.

We stood in single file outside the lodge with the Medicine Woman holding open the flap to the entrance. The dark sky above, dotted with stars, looked silently down. A chill in the air brought light quivers down our backs. Complete darkness reigned inside the enclosure. The only light to guide our steps came from the nearby fire pit, where glowing embers heated large rocks. These rocks, secured from a nearby mountain, are considered sacred to the First Nation's of the region. As these rocks have been in existence before humans, they are considered our elders. They listen to our pains and contribute to our healing. Once the rocks reach a level of intensive heat, they are placed in a pit that is built into the middle of the lodge. The contact of water on scorching rocks produces instant steam intended to penetrate our pores and extract the impurities from our bodies.

Standing in line with five other women, we would soon take our place inside the symbolic womb. I peered into the dark void beyond the flap of the temescal. Passage would mark the final stage of my gestation. Logic would purport that if one is to progress in this world and particularly in this society, one must move forward with a decisive step toward creating an identify of my own. On this day, taking that step forward meant accepting another truth,

> Liberating myself would require that I embrace a contradictive perspective of the world that contested all that I had previously accepted as truth. New truths must be learned.

This concession, on my part, meant acknowledging that I was direly mis-educated. My challenge meant reclaiming that which I did not know I didn't have. This was quite a conundrum. How does one know what one does not have? Furthermore, in search of what I didn't have, I had to determine where to find it while figuring out what it was I was looking for. Confusion was deeply imbedded in my psyche and I could only hope that there were answers for me at the other end of the birth canal.

Contractions Leading to Regeneration

There was a series of successive events prior to the night of my symbolic regeneration that led me to the open flap of the temescal. One of the events that served as a contractive force prompting me to step through the aperture was the occasion of my daughter's 15th birthday. Through the process of determining how to mark this occasion, I bore witness to my own understanding of self in relationship to the world. The manner by which we eventually choose to celebrate her 15th birthday concurrently became a marker and, more so, an open affirmation of my own identity.

What started as a Native cultural tradition related to rites of passage for a young woman at this stage of her life has been influenced by Spanish practices and summarily adopted in my community. This merging of customs would dictate that my husband and I hold what is referred to as a quinceñera, a coming of age ceremony. Some people compare this to a debutante ball in which a young woman, at the age of 15, is presented to her community. There is generally a mass at which the young woman offers flowers to the Virgen of Guadalupe and there is a formal presentation of the young woman. She is accompanied by 15 couples consisting of godparents and sponsors. The young woman at the center of this ceremony dons the attire similar to that worn by a bride at her wedding but the color of the dress varies depending on the preferences of the family. The men wear tuxes and the women formal gowns.

Some families stretch their finances to host this event in which a live mariachi, a disc jockey, a sit down dinner, and even limousines are provided. Funding of this event is often underwritten by the godparents and sponsors. At that time, I had just started my employment at the tribal college so while we considered the options as to how to mark our daughter's coming of age, we determined that we could either embrace the tradition of the quinceñera or mark her 15th birthday like any other year. We weighed the merits of our two choices against the backdrop of our own evolving identities and consciousness about the many truths to which we were coming to understand.

Neither my husband nor I had been raised with a clear connection or conscious awareness of our Native heritage. Largely, it was subsumed and denied. Yet, both of us knew that we were both genetically connected to different tribal groups, he to the Chiricahua Apache and I to the Purépecha. Both of our families had selectively acculturated in order to survive in the United States. Diminishing the markers that would make us targets was meant "for our own good." Subsequently, it was conveyed to us that claiming one's "Indian" heritage was not only disadvantageous but was also a source of shame. Within our own families and community, these messages were clear.

I vividly recall one evening when, as a child, I was playing under the summer sun and joyously jumping over a lawn sprinkler. It did not take much for my skin to turn several shades darker so by the time I entered my home to dry off, I was as dark as the rich Mexican chocolate that my family enjoyed drinking on cold winter nights. My Aunt Pam, my mother's sister, was paying us a visit on this particular evening. She had fair skin and features that would prompt people to tell her that she resembled the actress, Elizabeth Taylor. She was proud of this. When my Aunt Pam saw me this particular evening, she started to laugh. This was done in my mother's presence. I did not know why she was laughing as no one, I, my mother, or her, had said anything particularly funny. My mother, puzzled at the outburst, looked at her sister who exclaimed, "Look how dark she is!" She continued to laugh even more. My aunt's one and only daughter had inherited her mother's fair skin. My mother suddenly understood the explicitness and degrading message behind the laughter. She then turned to me with a look of mortification. At the time, I did not understand what was so funny and though I did not internalize the message, I was left to process this event many years after it transpired. Fortunately, I liked my dark skin and all that is associated with it.

Nonetheless, the messages of family and community were negating. Even with our obvious physical features that reveal Native roots, my husband and I would often be told by elders in our respective families, "We are full-blooded Spaniards." Despite these messages from our own family, my husband was aware that the tribal nation to which he had been culturally disconnected held a ceremony that marked the passage of a child to adulthood; their ritual was referred to as the "Changing Woman" ceremony. Neither of the other two options for marking our daughter's 15th birthday resonated for us, so we discussed this third option with her. She did not feel particularly drawn to the other options nor did she reject the idea of venturing into our indigenous heritage for this special occasion; she remained open to the concept and with us, we moved forward.

The woman who held open the flap to the Sweat Lodge had provided my connection to the alternative. She had referred me to Angelbertha Cobb, a woman affectionately referred to as Mama Cobb by those who know her. The name she was given at birth is Cozamayotl Xihuatlalli, which means Rainbow Woman of the Earth. This is how she is referred to by those who know her in her homeland of Central Mexico where Nahuatl is the primary language. I stand at the opening of the Sweat Lodge and reflect on my first encounter with who will be referred to out of respect as Elder Mama Cobb.

Rainbow Woman of the Earth

I first met Elder Mama Cobb at her home which was, at the time, located in the midtown section of Sacramento. Upon entering her home, I was immediately immersed in the sights, sounds, and scents of a rich heritage. The first image I saw upon entering her home was the picture of an incredible looking man dressed in full Mexica regalia. I was later told that this was Elder Mama Cobb's teacher, Señor Yescas. Everywhere I looked my eyes took in symbols of Mexica culture—feathers, head pieces, blankets, and items utilized for ceremonies. I was introduced to two other gentlemen at this meeting that was set up for our daughter, Lilian, to meet Elder Mama Cobb. One of the gentlemen who we met that day was her biological son, Guy, and the other gentleman who was also introduced to us as her son was Benjamin Torres, her understudy. Although I did not know the significance at the time, my daughter and I were both smudged upon entering the home. Benjamin conducted the smudging using copal, a tree resin. This was my introduction to a womb that not only provided nourishment but that also lent itself to healing the wound in my psyche and soul.

Over the course of the months that followed this initial meeting, I came to know why this full-blooded Mexica woman was living in our midst. Elder Mama Cobb was born on October 1, 1932. The Mexican nation derives its name from her nation, and their oral traditions are the source for the symbols on the Mexican flag. The knowledge that she holds about the Mexica people is not widely published nor lectured about. It is the perspective of those who have their own version of what transpired, historically, without the tainting of the conqueror's pen. Given the indigenous voice to which she represents, I would venture to say that the knowledge she holds would be viewed as unpopular and controversial to many. There is a reason for this. It is widely known that in the aftermath of conflict between nations that the victor earns the privilege to pen "his" story. The perspectives of those who lose the war also forfeit the right to tell their version of what transpired while losing the right to sustain their way of life.

Those who survive the forces of subjugating violence are, for generations to come, subjected to real and constant threat of physical violence for not complying with the oppressor's interpretation of events as well as their take on day-to-day reality. While I had personally not known physical violence in my lifetime, I had direct experience with violence of a different nature, the psychological and spiritual violence inflicted by the pen that follows the sword. For this reason, the privilege of learning Elder Mama Cobb's rendition of what life for Native people was like in the pre-Cuauhtémoc era became the salve by which the wounds of the violence would eventually heal. She provided truths that the conquerors and colonizers had attempted to erase and distort.

One of the earliest examples of the effort to malign the Indigenous people's written record is chronicled by what transpired in New Spain. Fray Bernadino de Sahagún (1499–1590), one of the earliest historians in the America's, drew from Indian informants who knew the meaning of the hieroglyphs that contained pre-Cuauhtémoc Mexican history. As the conquering Spaniards had destroyed many of the original hieroglyphs, the informants reconstructed the images and interpreted them to the historian. Sahagún recorded their version. Additionally, he drew from these informants, former Chiefs and elders of the Mexica tribe, the account of the Conquest "as they saw and felt it." Once this firsthand account was published, he was forced to "change the account of the events" with the intent to "hide certain facts" (Bordeaux, 1974, p. 16). This occurred in the 1500s. Similarly, during the 1800s, petroglyphs, pictographs, and rock sculptures created by California Indians were summarily dismantled and destroyed during the conquest and colonization. Modern day historians are left with putting together what pieces of truth that can be distilled from the distortions in order to provide fuller volume to the counter narrative.

This is why most people alive today would find Elder Mama Cobb's personal story compelling. Without question, it flies in the face of what has been transmitted from the Spanish conquerors and subsequent colonists who, instead of harmoniously and peacefully engaging the people of this land, were more invested in destroying and subjugating them. The three key weapons employed consisted of the sword, disease, and religion. Knowing what we know now about the destructive swath of Spanish conqueror's forces, the relative existence of Elder Mama Cobb, the embodiment of the Mexica heritage, in our midst today is nothing short of a miracle. Untainted by the defiling conqueror's pen, her existence and the purity of the truths she holds is attributable to the prescience of Mexica nation's Emperor, Moctezuma, almost 500 years ago that led to decisive action in order to preserve the culture.

Commonly known is that the Spanish soldier, Hernán Cortés, landed in the port city of Veracruz in 1519. As he and his soldiers made their way to what is now called Mexico City, Moctezuma foresaw eminent destruction upon his people. The initial encounter between the Spaniards and the Mexica reveals a clash of intentions and values that exists even today. The former was intent on taking and expanding, while the latter was invested in defending and surviving. This is where the story of the encounter, as we know it, takes a turn toward self-preservation.

Cultural values vary around the world. Differences in the values of the Mexica and the Spaniards could not have been more disparate during this period of time. These two groups of people not only spoke different languages but what was of value differed as well. For example, when the Spaniards asked of Moctezuma for his treasure, the Spaniards were referring to gold; that which was of "worth" to the Spaniards of that era. To Moctezuma, the "treasure," that which was of value for the Mexica, was not gold, it was the women, the children, and the elders of their nation. This is what Moctezuma sought to protect.

Prior to the arrival of the Conquistadores, the perceptive Emperor separated a small group of people from the larger community. This group represented his "treasure" and along with additional items of value-feathers, animals, and a few warriors to defend the contingency, they were sent to a remote area of the state of Puebla. This is a region closer to Veracruz, where the Totonac resided. After the Spaniards, in 1521, attacked the Mexica in their capital city of Tenochtitlán, they proceeded to subject the Emperor to relentless torture. The Spaniards demanded that Moctezuma give up the "treasures" but the Emperor refused to betray his "treasure," his people.

The Spaniards proceeded to destroy the Mexica stronghold and conquered what was previously known as the Mexica (Aztec) empire. What they did not know was that while they continued their quest for "treasure" which meant riches of gold and other metals and gems, Moctezuma's treasure established themselves in a region inaccessible and out of reach of the conquerors. Intentionally hidden in the mountainous region of Puebla, there are, to this day, close to 300 people from the original Mexica nation living as their ancestors did. Four hundred years after the establishment of this new Mexican community, Lázaro Cárdenas, President of Mexico from 1934 to 1940, made a good will gesture to Native nations still persisting in Mexico. He called for a representative of each Native nation to serve as cultural ambassador to the Mexican Republic. Cozamayotl Xihuatlalli, though only a child not yet six years of age, was selected as that representative from the surviving Mexica nation. Five hundred years after the initial point of contact between the Spaniards and the Mexica, Moctezuma's treasure still exists, thrives, and provides us with a source of cultural affirmation through Elder Mama Cobb, a descendent from this community.

Elder Mama Cobb, an ambassador for the Mexica nation, became the principal dancer in the Mexican National Ballet Folklorico. She taught the teachers of the instructors of La Academia de la Danza, which evolved to become Ballet Folklorico de Bellas Artes. Also, she performed on the stage of the National Mexican Palace and toured worldwide with the National Ballet Troupe on behalf of the Mexican as well as the Mexica nation. Dancing frontline in full cultural dresses, she caught the eye of a United States serviceman, son of a Comanche mother, who, with flowers and romance, convinced her to marry him. This is how she landed in California, where she raised an extensive family. Elder Mama Cobb continues to serve as ambassador of the Mexica people while teaching Mexica dance, culture, customs, and, the reason for my meeting her, the ceremonies that she presides over.

Past Meets Present

Elder Mama Cobb, though small in stature, stands tall in any crowd. At our initial meeting, my daughter and I spoke to this full-blooded descended ambassador of the Mexica people about our desire to mark Lilian's 15th birthday in a meaningful way. Since I was employed at the Tribal College, I was able to secure the Cultural Arts Center as the location in which to hold the ceremony. Elder Mama Cobb inquired as to what gift my daughter, Lilian, would offer at the ceremony. I communicated to her that Lilian sang at which she then asked,

"Britney Spears?"

I understood at that moment that I needed to be clearer in the meaning as to the extent of my daughter's training so I clarified,

"No. She is classically trained."

One of the songs that Lilian had previously performed was the Ave Maria. Since this was a song with European origins and often sung for Catholic ceremonies, I did not know if it would be offensive to Elder Mama Cobb if Lilian were to sing this particular song as her offering so I cautiously added,

"She sings Ave Maria. Would it be appropriate for her to sing this song as her offering?" To which she responded,

"What better song than one dedicated to our Mother?"

At the time I did not know what she meant by "Our Mother." At the moment, I figured I had at least not perturbed or annoyed her so I concluded it better not to say much more. Elder Mama Cobb agreed to preside over Lilans rites of passage ceremony and she instructed Medicine Woman, Regina Garcia, and Understudy, Benjamin Torres, to oversee Lilan's preparation for this life event. In the Mexica language, Nahuatl, this ceremony is called the Xilonen.

Preparation and Ceremony; Filling the Gaps of my Cultural Memory

Learning traditions that have been eradicated from our heritage requires being instructed not only on what we do but why we do it. First, we were taught that if a person is to engage in a time honored ceremony with full heart, then there are preparations leading up to the event. This particular ceremony, the Xilonen, is metaphorically symbolized by the corn as it is central to Native culture for its nourishment. The representation of the corn in this ceremony is by virtue of the analogous development and maturation of a young woman. Mr. Torres gave Lilian several sessions in which to learn specific dance steps that she would do at the ceremony at which time she would be accompanied by Danzantes, dancers of the Mexica tradition. A few days prior to the ceremony, we held a special dinner at the college. Regina presided over the dinner, at which time she smudged the food. Afterward, those in attendance at the dinner proceeded to the ceremonial grounds where she conducted a pipe ceremony. We learned that one puts their prayers and thoughts into the smoke, which are then carried to the Creator. A sweat was conducted afterward. All of this was with the intention of mindfully purifying the body and spirit.

Lilian was required to fast the two days prior to the Xilonen. She was allowed only water. During this time, Elder Mama Cobb made a simple cotton dress for Lilian to wear at the ceremony and we were instructed to purchase simple leather sandals that would be comfortable during the physical dance in which she had been instructed. Regina's daughter, Angela, made a beautiful crown consisting of fresh flowers for Lilian to wear on her head. The outfit, in its humble simplicity, was elegant.

Lilian with her Aunt Rosa Chamberlain @ Xilonen, July 28, 2002

Both sides of my husband's and my family contributed by setting up, bringing food, and serving our guests of which we had over 100 in attendance. Most had never attended such a ceremony, so it was not only a special day but it was novel in the eyes of those who had never had the privilege of attending a Xilonen. We were explicitly instructed not to serve alcohol and, as all the preparation leading to the ceremony reflected, alcohol has no place in sacred rites.

Tables for our guests were set up in two sets of rows on opposite sides of the Cultural Arts facility, leaving a large open space in its midst where Angela and her partner constructed an altar. Up until the opening of the ceremony, someone was appointed to protect the altar so no one would accidently step on items that had carefully been constructed for this special occasion. Our guests were instructed not to take photos or video record the ceremony. They would have the opportunity to do so after the rite was completed.

The altar, roughly described, consists of four candles situated at designated positions representing the East, the South, the West, and the North. Cornmeal is sprinkled on the ground in a circle that links

the four candles at the outer posts. An elaborate altar in the middle consists of flowers, candles, and other items representing the elements. Guests were invited to stand at the perimeter of the circle but not to cross into the demarcated ceremonial circle. Members of our family were placed at the ceremonial posts prior to the procession that marked the beginning of the ceremony. The situated cardinal points and the delineated circle represent what is known as the Xantotl. In North American nations, this is called the Medicine Wheel. The offered picture portrays the representational symbols and circle.

The Tlalpanehuetl, the Grandfather Drum, was positioned at the northwest corner of the circle. Mr. Torres entered the facility from the southeast point of the circle in full regalia. Elder Mama Cobb, also donning her full regalia, made her own entrance wearing a head dress that symbolized her status in her community. Benjamin went directly to the drum and Elder Mama Cobb to the station of the North. Lilian was third in the procession and remained at the altar that was situated at the center of the circle.

Mr. Torres began drumming and though it was only one drum, the thunderous sound filled the room with an energy that captured and held everyone's attention. Danzantes entered the ceremonial circle, dancing to the beat of the drum. They, too, were in full regalia and joined my daughter who stood at the center altar. They then faced the East, the place of men, and danced as an offering. At this post, represented by the element of fire, my brother, Henry Jr., and our son, Michael, gave Lilian words of advice.

Their counsel was that Lilian be selective about whom she chooses as a life mate and they further advised that she seek only the companionship of men who respect her. This would be the first of four counsels provided by family and witnessed by community.

Lilian and the Danzantes then rotated to the station of the South, the place of children and where the element of earth resides. They danced, once again, and this is where Lilian gave her offering and sang the Ave Maria. Afterward, her Aunt Margaret and cousin, Olivia, gave words of advice. This process was repeated as Lilian and the Danzantes shifted to the West, the place of women which is represented by the element of water. Her Aunt Cathy gave words of counsel at this post, ensuring that Lilian understood the role of women in our culture, to seek to be independent and to serve as the centerpiece of her family.

It was pointed out that in the circle of relationships within the Xantotl that all are equal. While men and women are situated at opposite sides of the circle, it does not mean that women's relationship to men is oppositional. Rather, they provide a balance to one another. Similarly, while children and elders are situated at opposite points of the circle, they are still in relation to one another. All four—women, men, children, and elders—are of equal value with all living things of the earth. Within the circle, respect is accorded for the diversity of gender identity and sexual orientation. Differences with the realm of humanity are viewed as natural variations on a continuum of possible identities. Subsequently, the spiritual path of "two-spirits" would indicate that there is a quest for active evolvement in which the spirit seeks a physical reality in the lifetime that would promote greater understanding.

Upon arriving at the final post of the circle, to the north, which is the station of the Elders and represented by the element of air, Lilian received counsel from my mother and father, Norma Lilia and Henry, Sr., as well as from Elder Mama Cobb. Lilian was advised to develop wisdom. Our guests were then seated and enjoyed a beautiful meal. Mementos symbolizing the rite of passage adorned the tables and guests were invited to take them home. Photos were then allowed to be taken. This was July 28, 2002. It was the first ceremony in which I witnessed Elder Mama Cobb enact her culture. I would soon learn that it would not be my last. I came to embrace another truth which was,

I would have to learn how to stand tall, like Elder Mama Cobb, and learn to speak truths.

On the heels of this momentous event, I reflected and compared what I had just experienced along with what I had heard of Indigenous culture and beliefs; the latter always being maligned with descriptions that were degrading. Yet, what I had witnessed and was learning refuted what I had been taught about the beliefs and practices. The source and reasons for the contradictions were now becoming apparent and for the sanity and sanctity of the next generation, I became more conscious of my own intentions.

Further Contractions: Uprooting Columbus

Liberation from a toxic womb required expelling the contaminants that infiltrated my "Being." Standing up to *that which I had previously accepted as truth* meant mentally extracting that which had been implanted in me years ago. Uncovering *true truths* meant plucking the source of the lies from the very roots. The seeds of these untruths were planted in me early in my childhood when I was indoctrinated with tales of The Nina, The Pinta, and the Santa Maria. I had been taught that these purveyors of the first Atlantic slave trade were responsible for bringing us *"civilization."* I was left to wonder as to the nature of such a "civilization" that captured and kidnapped tens of thousands of people from the Americas to be stuffed into the holds of Spanish and Portuguese ships and sold into slavery in Europe (Forbes, 1993).

The intentions and acts of those who brought such "civilization" were not questioned in our history books nor were the genocide, rape, and subjugation that followed. Furthermore, when there was anything said about the civilizations of those who were already here, it was, most certainly, not spun favorably when told by the conquerors. What is the psychological impact on a child of Native roots to be born into the physical world exactly 451 years after Columbus landed on the shores of what would later be named by others, "America?" With the possibility of 365 days in a year on which to be born, this coincidence of fate appeared like a bad joke. Yet, my "self" as a child adhered to the tales of the mariner who "sailed the ocean blue in 1492."

Immersed in a culture steeped in Columbus Day Parades, Columbus Day Sales, Columbus Holidays, and book reports and childhood drawings of the three ships of Columbus, I was *expected* to celebrate the arrival of this enslaver. Though only a child, I consciously intuited that my presence on this land was tolerated only to the extent to which I adapted to and embraced a reality that maligned my Indigenous heritage. When, where, and what I was expected to be was in relation to the subjugator.

As a child, one is not fully aware of all this. Subsequently, I had adapted to this illusory world and attempted to make sense of my presence in this false reality by inserting myself as creatively as I could. To stake my claim in this deceptive reality, I would proclaim, "I was born on Columbus Day!"

then, I would back up this proclamation with how I had arrived into the world on this most momentous day,

> *I came from a walnut that grew on a tree that is south of here. One day I fell off the tree and landed in a creek below. Protected by the outer shell I traveled on the water for many miles. I came to rest in Walnut Creek, California, and that is where I came out of the shell and so I was born there. (Borunda, 2010)*

Jarring myself out of this illusory connection took a lifetime's worth of travel as other narratives reveal. The silencing, the adapting, the submersion into someone else's trumped up reality were no longer working for me. The birth of my authentic self rather than a contrived self was just the beginning. My journey to a cleansed reality had just started on the day I stepped into the Sweat Lodge. After several hours of chanting, praying, singing, and sweating on October 12, 2003, I would no longer claim to be born on "Columbus Day." When I emerged from the temescal into the chill of the night and the blessings of the stars above, I made the declaration that the day of October 12th, the day of my physical birth and now my spiritual rebirth/regeneration would from that day on be called Indigenous People's Day.

How the Americas Discovered Europe

Almost eight years after emerging from the Sweat Lodge, my husband and I traveled to Ireland to celebrate our 30th wedding anniversary. While visiting points of interest in Galway's downtown area, I noted on the city map a "Columbus Monument." It was next to the River Corrib. We made our way across the city streets toward the river that flows from the Salmon Weir through the City of Galway and out into Galway Bay. It is important to note that Galway Bay faces the Atlantic Ocean which, on the other side, lays the American continent.

We found the small monument by the bank of the river just where the map stated it would be. It is not a particularly prominent monument. It is not incredibly large or ornate, but it is significant in that it refutes a long held belief that "Columbus Discovered America." In actuality, Columbus had traveled through Ireland in the late 1400s. While passing through Galway, he encountered hard evidence attesting to the fact that people from the Americas were in Europe. I was struck with the realization that I was following the footsteps of noted Professor Emeritus Jack Forbes. It was in 2008 that I had the privilege of hearing Professor Forbes speak at the University of California, Davis, about his 2007 publication "How the Americas Discovered Europe." This book offers evidence as to the capacity of people from the Americas to navigate the Atlantic Ocean currents that would carry them from the Americas to the European shorelines and back again.

Additionally, Professor Forbes discussed how in the margins of a book, Piccolomini's *Historia rerum*, Columbus wrote the following words in Latin, "People from Katayo came towards the east. We saw many notable things and specifically in Galway, Ireland, a man and wife" (p. 6). Further scribble written by Columbus that historians have attempted to decipher vary; however, the rest of his description of two people who hung to this boat and possibly carried to the shores of Galway as a result of a storm have been described as "superb creature" or possibly, "wondrous aspect" and finally, "of admirable form."

Columbus had evidence that there was life on the other side of the Atlantic. The "signs" of land beyond, however, were not people from Katayo (Cathy or China) as he had thought. Instead, these were people from the Americas who landed on European shores by use of masterfully built kayaks. On the monument is engraved the following,

On these shores around 1477, the Genoese Sailor Cristoforo Colombo
Found Sure Signs of Land Beyond the Atlantic.

Courtesy of Rose Borunda.

The monument was dedicated to the people of Galway by the City of Genoa, which is Columbus' place of birth. The "signs" that Columbus encountered on the shores of the River Corrib were people from the American continent. Despite the early discovery of Europe by Native Americans, there have been no attempts to dominate Europeans or make claim of the land. Yet, evidence speaks to realities subsumed and twisted over time. From this monument and from the insightful and progressive research and publications of scholars (Forbes, 2007; Loewen, 1995; Zinn, 1999) who are intent on bringing a multidimensional perspective to our reality, we can embrace a foundational truth.

Those of us with ancestors from America must reclaim our heritage in order to restore our inner wisdom and purpose so that we may heal.

References

Bordeaux, E. (1974). *Ancient America paradise lost.* San Diego, CA: Academy Publishers.

Borunda, R. (2010). Rebirth of the indigenous spirit: Turning the world right side up. In V. Sheared, J. Johnson-Bailey, S.A.J. Colin III, S.D. Brookfield, & Associates (Eds.), *The handbook of race and adult education: A resource for dialogue on racism* (pp. 31–42). San Francisco, CA: Jossey-Bass Publishers.

Freire, P. (1998). *Pedagogy of the oppressed.* New York: The Continuum Publishing Company.

Forbes, J. (1993). *Africans and Native Americans.* Urbana-Champaign, IL: University of Illinois Press.

Forbes, J. (2007). *The American discovery of Europe.* Urbana and Chicago, IL: University of Illinois Press.

Loewen, J.W. (1995). *Lies my teacher told me: Everything your american history textbook got wrong.* New York, NY: Touchstone.

Zinn, H. (1999). *A people's history of the United States.* New York: Harper Collins Publishers, Inc.

5

*Her*stories
of Decoloniality

Introduction

This weight on her back—which is the baggage from the Indian mother, which [is] the baggage from the Spanish father, which [is] the baggage from the Anglo?

—Anzaldúa, 2007, p. 104

Competing truths about colonizing and colonized cultures circulate through narratives or stories in schools and society. To counter those narratives that have been deeply rooted in colonialism, often represented as "truth" through a master narrative, it is vital to remember that no one can tell us that what has transpired in our cultural lives is not true; you have experienced it, lived it, cried over it, and even laughed in joy over it. You hold truths that have shaped and informed your own identity formation. You also have the possibility, the capacity, to create and reconfigure your own cultural narrative or "story" to a certain degree. As represented in the four interrelated cultural narratives written by Borunda, her life has been informed by cultural decisions made by her ancestors who faced

101

institutional structures of inequalities. Their sensibilities and dispositions, values and beliefs, and social positionality all contributed and shaped the normalized reality into which Borunda was born into and the ways she reconfigured her known reality. Overarching that reality, "*herstory*," is a cultural narrative about shifting her identity formation. Within this cultural narrative lies a persistent effort to define the self and that of future generations. She suggests that through colonization, one ingests the "master narrative," but there is also the possibility of culturally decolonizing oneself to a certain degree by forming cultural "counter narratives" for generations to come.

What follows in this chapter is a vibrant array of cultural narratives by authors who have explored and explained how they have deconstructed, interrogated, and negotiated multiple forms of colonization and racialization, and who have engaged in cultural processes of decolonization in their everyday life. Their narratives, as Chicana, Latina, and Amerindian women, are grounded and contextualized in their own network of relationships and power relations. We encourage readers to deconstruct the cultural and structural forces these authors illustrate, as well as identify their cultural agency, and their forms of resistance to domination. Notice how the authors of these cultural narratives represent the self as an empowered social agent who has survived and negotiated the effects of colonization, as well as transformed and created new meanings surrounding their cultural realities.

References

Anzaldúa, G. (2007). *Borderlands/la frontera: The new Mestiza* (3rd ed.). San Francisco, CA: Aunt Lute.

Coming Home to Danza

Jennie Luna

Ometeotl. I am a product of the Danza Mexica spiritual "movement." By movement, I draw upon the two meanings of "movement": the actual physical moving of the body and also a political, cultural, and social movement. In many ways, it was Danza that led me to an academic path and to become a lifelong learner. Some researchers who have studied the topic of Danza, also referred to as traditional Aztec Dance, write from the perspective of an academic arriving to this subject as an outsider. For me, it was the opposite experience. I arrived at the academy as a danzante. To be a traditional Mexica/Aztec dancer is more than a "cultural experience," but a metaphor for life. It was Danza that shaped my epistemology or way of knowing and it was the entrance, not only to my own sensibilities, dispositions of wisdom, and passion but also to a Native way of being. Danza, from the day I first stepped foot onto an institution of higher education, was part of my identity and the lens through which I viewed my academic experiences and made my personal choices. It has been my guide to living a harmonious, balanced, and spiritual path.

It was at one particular Raza Day event where I first heard of a woman, named Señora Angelbertha Cobb, who spoke with passion about Native knowledge. Raza Day is an event organized by the student organization Movimiento Estudiantil Chicana/o de Aztlan (MEChA) in efforts to encourage Chicana/o and Latina/o high school students to pursue higher education and become politicized, community advocates. Señora Cobb was the keynote speaker at this event, which took place at San José State University. She spoke about the need for all of us to stay connected to our Native heritage and that we no longer needed to learn "his"-story, but instead we had to reclaim "our"-story. She stated firmly that she was "Mexica," more commonly known as "Aztec," born in the highlands of Puebla, México, and her first language was Nahuatl. I remember very clearly going home and telling my mother about this woman and saying that she identified as an "actual" Aztec. I had learned in my own history books that Aztecs and other Native groups were extinct or something of the past. I knew that as a Mexican, I had "Aztec" in my blood, or at least that is what I was told or understood to be true as part of "Mexican" identity. But, I had no idea that "pure" Aztecs still existed; certainly she was one of the "last ones." At that point, I had no idea that my first encounter with this woman and this entire experience would transform my entire life and path. Señora Cobb, also affectionately called Mama Cobb, would become my maestra (teacher) and a key person in my life who would open doors for me not only in terms of Danza but, more importantly, would also encourage me to research and learn about the wisdom and history of my own Native people and roots—who I learned were the Caxcanes, the western Nahuas of the Zacatecas region.

When I began dancing in San José, California, to my knowledge, there were only two or three Danza groups that existed in San José at that time in the 1990s. Going to Danza, for many youth like me, was the first step to reclaiming "our"-stories and communities. What I remember clearly about my first Danza practice is hearing the drum and feeling a need to be there, as if it was where I had always belonged. This experience, of what I now understand as a manifestation of "genetic memory," is a powerful force that has continued to lead me down a path connected to my ancestors. Genetic memory is the overwhelming feeling of an immediate connection to an ancestral past or belief system, although never having experienced it firsthand. It is the idea that the memory of our ancestors sometimes exists below the surface, hidden in our genetic code, and is awakened when we are confronted with a profound experience that stirs our spirit.

While I acknowledge the ways in which my own spiritual growth was nourished by Danza, it was not devoid of challenges. Some Danza groups, including my first Danza group, gave me the impression that they were not interested in teaching women to play the drum, and in fact held on to scripted gender roles within Danza that did not honor my sensibilities or what I felt was truthful. I also noticed that there was little open or "out" space for Queer danzantes within Danza circles, despite the fact that there are many LGBTQ danzantes. Traditionally, LGBTQ, and those referred to as "Two-Spirit" in contemporary Native American beliefs, held important roles in the community and were revered and connected to the sacred. Native conceptualizations of gender were multiple and dynamic, yet within Danza circles, limitations were often positioned based on gender and sexuality. At the end of Danza practice, the circle is brought together for a closing prayer or palabra (word). In Danza, palabra holds a dual meaning. It is both "a word" or prayer and a responsibility simultaneously. To close the Danza circle, everyone would say in unison, "El es Dios!" (Translation: He is God!) It was voiced in a way that respected a higher being and was explained to me that before we humans speak, we acknowledge our Creator-God, known by many names: Great Spirit, Great Mystery, God, Dios, etc. I adopted this idea of El es Dios, using it in a similar way that "Amen" was used in my Catholic upbringing. I did not give much thought to this idea, other than the fact that at every Danza practice and ceremony, it became the scripted way that everyone responded. It was an experience at a MEChA National Conference, held at the University of California, Berkeley (UCB), that caused me to re-think this concept.

In 1995, I was a first year student in college and a young, budding MEChistA de UCB. Since I was new to the organization, I had not participated deeply in the organizing of the national conference. I arrived to the scheduled sunrise ceremony at César Chávez Park, located in the Berkeley Marina, more as a participant than as an organizer. When I arrived, I was the only MEChistA from UCB present and no one had arrived to lead the sunrise ceremony. Other MEChistAs from across the nation had made the early morning sacrifice to be there on time for the rising of the sun, and seemed frustrated at the lack of organization. Since I was the only UCB representative, I took it upon myself to get everyone in a circle. Flying by the seat of my pants, I pulled from my Danza knowledge and said that we should begin the morning with a "palabra." I began with the words, "El es Dios," and explained that in the Danza way, we begin our prayers with "El es Dios." I invited everyone to offer their palabra beginning from my left all the way around the circle, following the direction of our heart. As the palabra made its way around the circle, one by one, MEChistAs shared their thoughts, words, and prayers. Somewhere in the middle of the circle, one Chicana paused and said in a loud, firm voice, "Ella es Dios." I looked at her and smiled, the smile mostly meant for myself, because for some reason, the repeated verse of "El es Dios" had become so normative for me and it had never occurred to me that Ella es Dios (She is God) too. When the ceremony leaders finally arrived, they began to set up the fire in the center and invited me into the center of the circle, offering me the opportunity to join them, in what would be my first pipe ceremony, as a way to thank me for helping create the circle that morning.

This moment impacted me as I began to question the patriarchal notions that dictated even my own perceptions of God and how a "male God" could be manifested through me, a woman. When I would visit my first Danza group, I began to notice the patriarchal manner in which the group operated and the privilege that was given to men and women who were complacent in the patriarchal structure. I noticed this, especially as I started taking Chicana Studies classes that were exposing me to critical thinking through Xicana Feminist theory. I observed my own cousin, a male, who I had brought into the Danza tradition, being given special privileges, regalia, and access to certain parts of Danza that I knew I would never be nurtured into if I remained in this group. Even the historical narrative of the origins of Danza in the United States has been credited overwhelmingly to men, ignoring the contributions of women such as Señora Cobb. Oftentimes, the role of women in Danza has been relegated to the "partner," "wife," or "participant," but never the leader. Even when women have been given palabra or the responsibility of care-taking a Danza group, their leadership role has been delegitimized or overlooked when the time came to seek knowledge or ask questions. It was assumed that the "authentic" knowledge keepers had to be the men, when in fact, in most Native pueblos, it is the women who keep the fires burning; understand the uses of sacred medicines; and keep traditions, language, and spirituality alive in the home. It is because of Native women ancestors who resisted colonization through the preservation of cultural/ spiritual ways that a people who were not meant to survive, now thrive.

A new generation of Danzantes and activists are emerging with a mujerista politic and woman-centered spirituality. Younger danzantes have replaced the words, El es Dios, with Ometeotl, a Nahuatl word that translates as Ome: two and Teotl: energy. The term *Ometeotl* is an acknowledgment of a Creator Life force that is dual, both feminine and masculine. This concept resonates within me, as I too am a reflection of that Great Spirit that holds both feminine and masculine energies within my one body.

Danza and the Xicana/o Movement was my turning point and moment of (trans)formation. These movements not only changed me ("transformation") but also were a critical part of my "formation" as a human being, critical thinker, and organizer. Coming to my own Native knowledge, encoded in my very being, in the genetic code contained in my hair, blood, and skin, is the process of reclaiming memory and being reminded that I carry my ancestral legacy everywhere I go. It is my birthright to have voice, to belong, to own my feminine power, and it is my right to pray. Danza has been the answer to my prayers and has led me to this moment in time, to this palabra, *Ometeotl*.

Daughter as Caretaker: Living the Four Directions

Maria Mejorado

We are a family of four. This family configuration is a conscious decision on my part to have a husband, a son, and my father all in the same home. I am told, this represents the balance of the Xantotl in which the man is represented in the place of the East, the woman in the West, children in the South and the Elders are in the North. This was not always what I imagined would be my family configuration but it is now what we live and do our best to honor in our every day lives. Being the youngest and only daughter in a family of six brothers has not been easy. All my life I have been expected to take care of my parents, a notion I resented and fought against and which is now being tested.

My early training as a caretaker were well in place by age four as I recall rushing to help my Dad as my Mom quickly tied the long grapevines into a neat braid, and then quickly move onto the next plant in the agricultural fields of the Central San Joaquin Valley, leaving my father behind. I don't recall what prompted that response other than working the long rows of grapes was best done side by side. By Junior High, I washed my Dad's socks by hand and from time to time and in a jealous tone, my Mom retells the story. Her jealousy was subtle and stinging yet understandable given that Dad was a much better father to his only daughter than a husband to his wife.

Upon graduating from high school, I was accepted to attend a private catholic college that was located 150 miles away from home. One of my brothers disowned me because he thought it was my role to take care of my parents. It was ironic that he upheld this family role for me given that he was in a much better position to care for my parents' needs since he lived near my parents, was married and settled, while I was just launching on my own as a college student. He did not speak to me for several months.

The first most challenging caretaking role imposed upon me took place as a young adult, with the first college degree in the family in hand, following a short visit, and against my protests, my father left my mother with me. He wanted his freedom. My mother described the ending of their 41-year marriage as being thrown out like a stray cat. A short time following the divorce, he moved in with Teresa, a neighbor who replaced my mother and took care of him for the next 20 years, but not without having her own set of complaints. She suddenly died six years ago. Since then, my father had been living alone, with occasional family visits and limited telephone calls. Ten years ago, Teresa first shared her concern about my father's memory loss and unexpectedly asked me if I would ever place my father in a nursing home. This caught me by surprise as I stumbled for a reassuring response to her question.

My father's diet was reduced to whatever he could purchase at the 99 Cent Only Store since it was much easier to pay given his progressing dementia and purchased mostly frozen foods like TV dinners and muffins. He continued to work in a European motor garage, and was fortunate that his employer had a big heart and wouldn't fire him even as his driving became more erratic and he had difficulty remembering the directions to drive customers home. The guys at the shop became his family and protected Dad as his language skills became less comprehensible and his driving more erratic. Most telling of their tolerance and love of my father was their patience with him as he was dropping in the shop four or five times a day to see if they needed anything. Following that conversation, I hung up the phone and cried as I realized that Dad had long lost much of the connection with me and my brothers. I also cried when the neighbor told me Dad was robbed by a couple he met at the local 99 Cent Store. They asked him to drive them to his apartment because they needed to use the bathroom. I was surprised that the neighbor was apologetic by my reaction, when she herself was the full-time caretaker of her own mother who had full-blown Alzheimer's disease.

It wasn't helpful that he lived six hours from me, yet I escorted him to Teresa's funeral in Mexico and spent days going through her things which stubbornly held her energy and scent and was too painful for my Dad without her physical presence. My hands were swollen with handling hundreds of boxes stacked from floor to ceiling from 7:00 am to 10:00 pm every day for 10 days. My husband called daily asking when I would be returning home. While Dad trusted me going through her things, he stubbornly refused to leave his home, his job, or his community.

Teresa loved children and although she did not have any of her own, she would have been thrilled when we were offered a baby boy to adopt. My family didn't express much sentiment about our decision to adopt except for my mother who was most vocal against the idea. As I write this, I wonder whether her opposition was her concern that my role as her caretaker would be compromised or that having children was a biological event, not a conscious choice to raise someone else's child.

Joy in parenting was not something I experienced in my family, which may be the reason it was not a role I aspired to until I reached the age of 42.

After four miscarriages, the question became, how important is it that the child be biological? Another four years quickly passed as I fully engaged in my new career as a college professor, negotiating a highly political and at times hostile environment within my department. After a year of being in the system, and with no offers in sight, we decided to embrace being a "childfree family", then I received a phone call, from the adoption agency's office in Los Angeles. The birthmother interested in us was smart, engaging, and funny. More importantly, she did not come from a troubled background nor was she engaged in any substance abuse, a compromise we had come to expect. Our 11-year interracial marriage and our education were key to sealing the deal and we hit the jackpot! Joaquin has given us so much joy over the last four years and my mother is equally enchanted with him as he is with her!

Last year, in an effort to support Dad's independence, I coordinated a home assessment meeting to ascertain in-home support services. To my disappointment, he refused services. Had he become paranoid and less trusting of strangers, especially after being robbed trying to help others? So without this daily support, leaving Dad in his community was not an option. Knowing that Mom continues to rant about Dad's shortcoming to anyone willing to listen (30 years after the divorce), I casually mentioned to her that I was considering moving Dad to our area. She became very angry and pointed out all the reasons why he shouldn't. She was right, but I wonder if having my Dad closer to me, once again, could threaten my role as a caretaker for her or was it the unresolved feelings, he still harbored against him? To everyone's surprise, she recognizes that he is not the same man, as his illness progresses and withholds her usual rhetoric.

There was a decision of synchronicity and serendipity that we experienced. At a family meeting to explore Dad's options, we wondered how long Dad had been living alone. I opened my date book and I saw that our family meeting was taking place exactly six years to the date of Teresa's sudden death. This was a sign that we were honoring her by gathering to bring my father back into the family fold.

When my father was asked who he would like to live with, he pointed to the son who lives 90 miles away and who had been attending to my Dad's needs and calling him every day for the last six years. My brother walked out clearly upset for he was more than willing to take him but couldn't. So my husband, being the emotional caretaker in the family, stepped in and offered my dad our home. While this was a gallant gesture, it perplexed me. He immediately took me aside and shared that he misspoke in an effort to save my brother from being devastated and that he was highly concerned about me given the responsibility of raising our four-year-old son, my job as a professor and as a director of a federally funded program, my marriage, and mother's medical needs. How would this affect us?

My husband reluctantly consented to have dad move into a fifth wheel on our property, which would give him his own space and us the level of privacy we had become accustomed to. I was relieved that my husband supported what I felt was my duty. It seemed to be working well as Joaquin started hanging out with his grandpa in "La Trailita," which gave us a little respite. I wanted so much to get Dad integrated into the community and I connected him to a local Food Closet on Tuesdays at 6 am. I also found a welcoming Spanish speaking Senior Center on Wednesday mornings and escorted him to regular medical checkups for medication, something he had refused his entire life. Once this was all accomplished, I felt exhausted.

While my husband is having to constantly maintain La Trailita's propane, sanitation, heating and cooling systems, something that is becoming a daily chore, Joaquin enjoys spending time with his grandpa watching children's videos and recognizes our family as four members. However, as my dad gets tired or anxious, he is more apt to become short, something my son is not accustomed to nor do we like to see.

It is difficult to see my father's cognitive and physical abilities slipping away. Equally painful and most challenging is seeing the depth of his emotional needs. On our way to his favorite 99 Cent Store, he declares in Spanish "I've been thinking". "What about Dad?" I ask . . . . . silence . . . . . . "You've been thinking about what Dad?" "It's my fault," he says . . . I tried three times to find out what he felt bad about and never got a clear answer. But he looked sad then and days later.

What helps ease my guilt of moving Dad from his community is my understanding that he lost many of his cognitive skills long before he came to live with us, and took care of himself mostly by rote memory. The challenge I now face, much sooner than expected, is finding the level of support for him to be safe and happy. My husband supports and reminds me that there are acceptable limits to the role as caretaker regardless of our cultural expectations and upbringing. I may be finally learning my lesson finding balance in my roles as mother, wife, professional and daughter. In the meantime, as my four year old son acknowledges we are a family of four; me, my husband, our son, and now the elder, my dad.

Honoring Ancestors and Decolonizing Lessons

Michelle Maher

There are lessons about decolonizing myself that I have been blessed to experience in my life. At the same time, I am careful to discuss all of these lessons and how my Native people, elders, and I know how to survive in the Western world. Our and other ancestors foresaw that walking in balance, in right relationship with all that is during this time, would be challenging.

They were given ceremonies that remind us of sacred ways of living and these ways must be protected. One reason I am careful is for the protection of the ceremonies that teach us sacred ways of living. It is well-known that Native ceremonies used to be illegal. Some ceremonies predating the United States had to go underground or disappear. In addition, some people who attend Native ceremonies continue to be discriminated against by those who do not understand and those who think they are accepting of cultural differences but are not. So, even though the lessons involved in many ceremonies are truly available to all people, this climate is a social context in which many who attend ceremony live. We pray for the protection of these ways that bring us "home," heal us, and keep us living together in a good way. Future generations were considered by our ancestors. They formed ceremonies to remind us of natural law. These sacred ways include rather obvious ways to live together, like being kind and respectful to each other and especially elders—those who have developed wisdom during their lives. Elders come first so we can thank them for showing us how to live. Therefore, we listen to each others' experience with compassion. Many of these natural laws are on the front page of the paper such as to avoid polluting the water we drink.

Representing these lessons are challenging. The contemporary importance of tribal sovereignty need not get entangled with representing one by their ancestral lineage. Often in Indian Country, people are introduced by their First Nation, American Indian, and/or Alaska Native affiliation only. By honoring all of my ancestors, I respect the sovereign governments that represent my ancestors' relatives who were forcibly put on reservations, whereas my ancestors left. For myself, personally, representing my identity is complicated. My mom identifies as Cree, Blackfeet, French, English, and German. My father is Swedish and Tsalagi. My stepfather is Irish. In the Native American tipi ceremony tradition in which I participate, we are all family regardless of blood ties. Highlighting someone's adoption is disrespectful. Some of these ways of identifying do fit simply into the categories that have become a product of colonization. I have learned to honor all of my ancestors because walking in balance requires it. My mother and other tribal elders encouraged my sister Stacey and me to walk the Red Road: to follow American Indian traditional ways of living in balance while also living in Euro-American dominated places. Walking this Red Road can be challenging. It is impossible to avoid interfacing with the Western cultural and economic world. It is challenging because colonized ways of being with others can be difficult to identify. For example, to stay in academia, I have had to follow its rules of advancement and status. To be decolonized, I know that such advancement and status means nothing beyond what I can share willingly.

My mother and sister have aided my decolonization process. My mother, Maryann, is an elder who participates and sets up ceremonies intended to decolonize us. She has helped me gain a native voice by teaching me by example. I love and admire her. As an elder she has an empowering vision of being an elder, following the example and activity of the Thirteen Native Grandmothers. They are grandmothers from throughout the world who have come together to be a collective and to empower the voice of living in balance and taking care of our environment as well as taking care of all of our relations. Also, my incredibly funny sister, Stacey, and I have benefited from many traditions that are in our areas that have brought us "home." For example, Stacey prepared her prayer ties and spent four days and nights without food or water under the watchful eye of a Lakota elder and friend. She has spent years training and now pours (water) in the sweat lodge for her family and community. Here in our backyards, we come to pray much in the same form as 10,000 years ago, except we have washing machines for the blankets and chain saws for the wood and refrigerators for our meal. I am so incredibly blessed by my sister.

These Native ceremonies remind me of what is important in everyday life. Participating in these ceremonies has kept me from investing in the forms of Western culture that make me feel like an indentured servant. They remind me that the right relationship does not have to do with any of the things the Western world is centered upon: power, money, status, and what you look like. For example, this happens when one by one we crawl on our hands and knees to remind us of where we came from. A sweat lodge is a small east-facing willow structure on the ground that people sit within. Grandfather stones that have been heated by the fire are brought inside. We sit and pray together in the dark, where we can clear our minds and experience our hearts together. Sometimes the ceremony is held within a tipi. One way a tipi is put up is with four initial poles that represent the four directions. The poles also remind us that the four races of humanity went in the four directions. I have heard it said that this ceremony is tied at the top because we were told that the four races would come together some day. These ceremonies help put fear in its place. Western culture and public education seem to be based upon instilling many fears, fears of being judged in a way that one will be excluded, lose access to their community, and means of survival and luxury. Because of the power of education, I became interested in how schooling can help facilitate a social context where young people might experience more giving and supportive relationships with each other. Ceremonies are places where I refocus on what matters, especially such matters of the heart. I am reminded that what is real is our connection to Creation; to these traditions and our medicine; to the water, earth, air, and fire; and to ourselves, friends, family, and all life. Afterward, we share food, a form of prayer, and share our stories. In this beautiful context, we form our relationships.

Sometimes I get caught up in the pressures of Western life, mainly fear what others think and the potential consequences of that for my everyday relationships. These ceremonies help me remember to live and make changes here in the present, informed by how people might operate, but not be controlled by that. While I know it is possible to feed and safely house humanity, the worries of being unemployed, struggling to provide for our families, to teach traditions, and fearing for our relatives, children, and elders can distract us from enjoying the present and being thankful for it. I have learned that Creation, not people, is in charge. I am not in control and to seek control is a dangerous endeavor in relationships because what is gained through power destroys trust. Instead we all have a place, like any other life form. We all belong. Connection is built upon caring and sharing, not power. Connecting to my environment helps me navigate because then I am more in touch with myself and others as a guide in the present.

This connection happens with sitting up all night praying with my family—as we are all family in this ceremonial way—and is the most important time of my life. In our traditions, everyone is welcome. For example, Mexica people have been attending these ceremonies for a few years now. They have invited me to the Danza, to pray in traditional dance, the dance-prayer of their ancestors. What a good time we have together. We share our people's ways with each other with respect. These ways have much in common which means that I must not assume the meaning. The connection that we share shows me that these ways of praying together are rooted in being a family. Ultimately, being a part of each other's family and Native ceremonies transforms the people in those ceremonies. This is a way of coming back together that makes me smile. We are coming together. Yet this does not mean that we change the ways that certain things are done. We pass on the ceremonies in the ways they were passed to us, in order to maintain their integrity. At this time of the Great Coming Back Together, there are pointers to the way home that begin in our hearts and are shown in our actions.

What I have learned sitting up in tipi meetings, sweats, and elsewhere is to experience how we are all connected. Forgetting or distancing from our connection and intimacy with this life world, in any way, whether a person, an idea, a sexuality, disconnects me from my own heart, breath, and loved ones. Instead of disconnecting, I am learning to be curious and investigate. For example, decolonization means finding the place of our two-spirit brothers and sisters when we may have lost the understanding of the sacred lessons they bring in who they are. How I sustain myself is to experience my connection to all that is, all those I know and love, my friends, family, and ancestors. I remember that the spirit that looks through my eyes is, at its essence, the same as the one that looks through yours. It does not mean that you experience the world as I do. This, I believe, is the sacred invitation to get to know my spirit in you and your spirit in me and in All That Is. Such a perspective reminds me to consider how to be with those that do not realize they are separated or those that do and do not know how to come home. It offers me compassion.

When I am on my knees praying during the ceremony, I remember that this is the time of the Great Coming Back Together. I pray about our future. People have their own paths home. How I respect what is in my heart of hearts has an effect on the outside world. A lesson related to medicine is having a prayer answered when you ask to be shown what we hold on to that is no longer useful—maybe a burden we carried from our own naiveté about how to deal with circumstances we have faced or are facing. I have recognized how I have held on and been taught to hold on to fear, despair, trauma, and shock in order to take care of my "self." One's identity is a target for colonization. I feel blessed to have been shown where my mistakes were and to unwind bearing the burden of circumstances I have experienced. I learned that experiencing difficult things does not actually separate us from ourselves, others, our world; however, those illusions that can make us feel like there is a barrier. I am a beneficiary of sacred medicine that felt like it altered the course my life.

A Cinco de Mayo Birth: Finding Myself in Yesterday

Julie Figueroa

I was born on Cinco de Mayo 1969 a few minutes after 6 am. When my mother tells me the story of my birth, there is a mixture of joy and unresolved anger in the tone of her voice. Even with this, I enjoy listening to the story of my birth. It's not so much that I like hearing about myself. In fact, anyone who knows me well would agree that I am uncomfortable with being the center of attention. Rather, listening to this story has a powerful impact on the way I think about my life. Vive con propósito (live with purpose) is something my parents always told their children. For me, how I was born and when I was born gave me the foundation to believe I have a responsibility to live with purpose.

There are four children in my family; I am the third in birth order. Given my father's transnational labor history prior to my being born, he was working in the United States when my mother gave birth to my two oldest siblings in Mexico. By the time I came, my parents were permanently living in San Jose, California.

Because my mother already knew how many contractions it took before each of my siblings arrived, she alerted my father that it was time to head to the hospital when I was going to be born. In an effort to keep my mother calm, he reassured her that everything was going to be fine. My mother, on the other hand, knew better given that this would be her third time giving birth.

My mother knew that the hospital was too far and that I was on the verge of joining my family. She asked my father to pull the car over near the firehouse on King Road, the street down from my family's house. After parking the car along the curb, my father ran to the front door. He pounded on the door wanting to get the attention of the firefighters inside. My mother remembers that a group of firefighters, still in their pajamas, ran toward her. By the time my father and the firefighters arrived, I was already born and it was Cinco de Mayo. I was happy to be a stubborn Taurus that day.

Like the gritos associated with Cinco de Mayo, I let out my own grito that day to celebrate my triumph of being born in spite of one doctor's intentions. Nine months prior to my being born, my mother was not feeling well. She visited a local doctor who prescribed some medication to make her feel better. As the months progressed, my mother felt worse. During one of those full days of working in the agricultural field, an elderly woman who worked alongside my mother asked her how she was feeling. My mother expressed that she was feeling extremely tired. In response, the elderly woman looked at my mother and in a matter-of-fact voice said, "You're pregnant, that's why you don't feel well." My mother was stunned because the doctor had prescribed birth control pills to address what was impacting her health. I struggled health-wise for about a week after being born to the point that a blood transfusion was necessary for me to survive. My mother was a perfect match to be a donor. My mother gave birth to me, and, extended my life. Much like the Battle at Puebla (also known as Cinco de Mayo), I was fighting for my life and, eventually, won the opportunity to live my life. I was coming to live with a purpose is how I see my birth.

Certainly, I question the doctor's motivation for prescribing birth control pills given that my mother clearly didn't realize she was pregnant at the time she began to consume the pills. While it's difficult to fend off the idea that my mother was the target of some eugenics agenda given the politics of the day, the fact that I survived overshadows any political agenda, but does not erase the possibility of a different outcome.

Growing up with Cinco de Mayo being my birthday always guaranteed a good time. My birthday is never one I associate with material gifts. Although we didn't have lots of money growing up, I felt completely wealthy when it came to amazing family memories. For instance, my parents took us to the lively Cinco de Mayo parade in downtown San Jose. For Dad, attending the Cinco de Mayo parades year after year was not just about understanding the beautiful Mexican traditions expressed through art, music, and food, but he also wanted me learn some Mexican history.

Namely, Cinco de Mayo has nothing to do with Mexican Independence, but rather Mexico's defeat of France. On the other end of the spectrum, attending these parades was also about imparting the cultural value of collective well-being within the Mexican tradition. My mother and father always talked about how people would visit the plaza to meet up with friends, visit that special person they liked, or spending time with family. The parade was a way for their children to understand that gathering as a people was not just a ritual defined by festivities, but a way of life.

In the end, my Dad made me feel like that parade in the downtown streets of San Jose was celebrating me too. He wanted me to feel special not just for being born, but to recognize that being born on Cinco de Mayo was somehow significant given the fact that I survived a difficult birth. With this history, Vive con propósito (live with purpose) are words that have become a way of life for me. I make every effort to exercise courage to move outside of my comfort zone to find my purpose in life.

In the journey to find my purpose, I moved away to attend college and complete my graduate school. Although I completed all my schooling in Northern California, my parents often describe me using the following phrase: Candil de la calle, oscuridad de tú casa (You are the light in the streets, the darkness in your house). Needless to say, my parents sometimes find it challenging to locate me at home given that I am out living my purpose. Another interpretation of the saying would be that to find purpose required that I confront and navigate borders as discussed by Chicana Writer Gloria Anzaldúa. Mostly, these were institutional borders that were not always ready to offer an equitable education or accept a low-income, first-generation Chicana. While navigating those borders was not always easy, I relied on lessons about personal strength, personal leadership, dignity, humility, and collective sense of well-being to give me the courage to ask for help, appreciate receiving help, and help others. As a Chicana, I find myself today by remembering and appreciating the struggles and victories that define my past.

To this end, reflecting on my lived experiences, who I have become, and the fact that I was born on Cinco de Mayo, I now find myself contemplating the rhetorical question with great appreciation from my friend and colleague, Gloria: "How much more Chicana can you get?"

Curls, Frizz, and Locks: A Latina Hair Story

Angie Chabram

In 2011, Anne Matheson published a book called Love My Hair. The cover features a brown-haired girl looking in the mirror, arms outstretched, celebrating her hair, with a teddy bear at watch. On the next page, a caption reads: "Some people might think Emily's life is ordinary. They might think her hair is ordinary . . . or too curly . . . or frizzy. Not Emily . . . Emily gets up early, looks in the mirror and sings, "I love my hair . . . It's big and it's curly . . . ." (Matheson, 2011, pp. 1–4).

My hair story stands in marked contrast to Emily's, which is organized around a singular expression of unconditional love and self-acceptance. My hair story is embedded in shifting personal narratives that suggest an interplay between body, self, family, and community. Rather than accepting my big curly, frizzy, unruly hair, I've made peace with it, and I will continue to do so even though others may not (Nikki, 2012). You see in American society the hair wars are raging all over the media as well as our bodies and self images[1] (Owns, 2002). These wars are premised on the idea that (Afro Latina) hair like mine must be straightened, curled, managed, and tamed so the Euro American ideal of white beauty and cultural citizenship (straight hair) can be upheld (Mercer, 1990). No wonder a recent blogger who was fed up with the negative attributes assigned to curly hair uttered, "Curly hair is an ideological position."[2]

Making peace with my curly, frizzy hair in the midst of this war and its normative standards has been a life-long process. I've had many detours and struggles. My hair and I have morphed into different hair-dos and don'ts, and we've taken different positions along the way. I've also embraced a variety of cultural aesthetics and codes, some "popular," others "alternative." As a young child, I sported what can be called a no-frills short Latina natural with bangs. My curls sprang forth but were suspended in mid-stream. I don't remember exactly when my cropped hair was abandoned, but in early elementary school, I already wore a ponytail that was later cut in preparation for my first communion. The ponytail was so precious to me that I later saved it in my top drawer. I liked to take it out and play with it and pretend I still had long thick curly hair that hung down to my shoulders and tapped my back. On occasion (and much to my sister's horror), I would cut my doll's hair in my attempt to satisfy a burgeoning sense of personal style and imitate the big Latina girls who tended to hair matters in our admittedly stylish working-class neighborhood.

At school, I noticed that girls and boys traded sometimes longing, wistful looks at the golden heads that were crowned with straight hair. Sadly, the kids would try to straighten their hair to no avail. They did

---

[1]See Wade in Kitchen Tales: Black Hair and the Tension between Individual Subjectivity and Collective Identity at http://sitemaker.umich.edu/intersections .cultural.studies/_black_hair_
[2]Recovering Fed, 2012.

the curl-free, the ironing, the blow-drying, and even the Puerto Rican do-be-do.[3] In retrospect, these experiments with hair straightening, which were laden with negative social meanings, were clear evidence that our hearts and souls were already conscious of the "burden of beauty" (Caldwell, 2000, p. 275). This was especially the case for those of us like me whose hair became a metaphor "for an entire race of people" (Caldwell, p. 275). But it was the lesson I learned on the street and not in the classroom that really drove home the weight of this burden to me.

The occasion was a visit to the beauty shop that was prompted by my upcoming crowning of the Virgin Mary in the May procession at St. Joseph's Catholic Church on Temple Street. In preparation for the procession, I was treated to the local beauty shop to have my hair professionally "done." The trip to the beauty shop was well worth it. I was thrilled by the beautician's work on my full head of unruly hair. She created a fluffy mid-chin flip with high bangs that looked like the hairdo of the outgoing twin on the 1963 "The Patty Duke Show."

When I looked in the mirror, I was amazed at what had been accomplished: Every strand of my hair lay in its rightful place as a result of the gobs of hairspray that threatened to choke the air. I was so proud! Filled with delicious anticipation, I waited on the curb for my brother to pick me up. I dreamed about how my family would react to the "new" me. But these dreams were rudely interrupted by the taunts of white teenaged boys who sped by, yelling at the top of their lungs. "Hey, you beaner!" they shouted. Startled, I wondered who this *you* was. I looked around the block, only to discover that I was the only person on the sidewalk. Sadly, I answered yes, they were yelling at *me*.

Within a matter of seconds, I went from unbridled pride and joy to the depths of humiliation. Mortified, I felt the gut-wrenching splitting of self, described so well by Frantz Fanon. I also wondered if I was being called names because the beautician had teased my hair too high or because I was being called Mexican—or both?[4]

Even as I felt personally targeted, I knew that Mexican Americans were often the subjects of name-calling in this city where neighborhoods were segregated by race and nationality. As I explain in my regional

---

[3]This was something I learned in Puerto Rico and taught to my friends. First, you'd find two orange juice or soup cans that were appropriate to the length of your hair. Then, you'd use them as rollers on the top of your head. Then, you'd create a turban with the rest of your hair, brushing it straight all around and pinning it down with long bobby pins.
[4]I provide a more in-depth discussion of this event and my autobiographical context in my essay, Growing up Mexirican in *Latino Studies*. 2009. 7:378–92.

autobiography: "Back then I wasn't aware of the extent of derogatory speech at some public school settings in La Puente, or that in Mexicans had faced exclusion from public facilities and could not "go to uptown La Puente and get their hair done or get a haircut" (Ochoa, 1984, p. 55).[5]

At the moment I heard the ugly words, I was angry but I was also ashamed. This perplexed me. I had to figure out whose shame I was experiencing. Was it mine for being who I was or theirs for being bad? I composed myself and was able to begin the process of healing my scar when I concluded that they (the ones who called me ugly names) should be ashamed. They delighted in being hateful. Truth be told, before I composed myself, I had already put water on the styled hair so it would flatten out a bit. I didn't want to make things worse and look like the Pachuca they were making me out to be.

But it wouldn't always be this way. As an undergraduate student at Berkeley, I staged the beginning of many hair rebellions. I let it grow long and natural, did the wash and wear, and embraced the unruly curls and frizz as a sign of my personal and political liberation. There was no need for a beautician, hair products, or primping. It was what it was—y que? Besides, the image of the liberated Chicana always featured women with long wild hair, even though the mane was usually straight and not curly like mine.

While professorship brought a more tame hair-do, the long-locks remained more or less constant in the form of the in-your-face chongo and the tightly braided single or double tails that resembled those of my youth. Once in a while, I also did the long straight hair-do I mastered while in Spain on the Junior Year Abroad Program, but the curly, frizzy hair always reemerged.

It wasn't until around May of the year 2009 that things changed dramatically. That's when I literally did a Frida, staging my own version

---

[5] I also explain, "Clearly, there was a larger history I needed to learn in order to understand how Mexicans had come to form the bottom of the city's social pyramid. I would eventually find out that this bigger history dated back to Spanish colonization and the founding of the San Gabriel Mission (1771); to the secularization of the region; and to the appropriation of the greater Rancho La Puente by Anglo rancheros who came west (1845) in search of cheap land and wealth. These rancheros received land grants (title) from the Mexican government (1845) for the 48,790-acre Rancho La Puente in order to launch lucrative agricultural and ranching enterprises using Mexican and Native American labor (for more on the history of the town, see the La Puente Valley Community History website: http://www.colapublib.org/history/lapuente). Distinct social hierarchies coalesced as these and other "European Americans." See Growing up Mexirican in *Latino Studies*. 2009. 7:378–92.

of mid-life Chicana resistance, affirmation, and recovery. Remember the movie? Frida committed the ultimate transgression by chopping off the long locks that often symbolize the Mexican woman's heterosexual beauty after she endured a particularly egregious heart break at the hands of her lover, Diego (Kahlo, 2012). She captured the connection between long hair and love in the patriarchal heterosexual mind-set in her self-portrait, where she explains in the movie: "Look, if I loved you it was because of your hair. Now that you are without hair, I don't love you anymore." (Taymor, 2002)

With her hair cut, she disposed of her lover's preference and affirmed her always present masculine side, which she emphasized with a gray suit and her bisexuality. In my case, it was all about getting rid of the old aesthetic, making plenty of space for letting the new feminine life grow. There was no alcohol and no personal ritual in my case. (Frida had her own paranda con canción y todo when she cut her hair.) I left the whole business of cutting up to the beautician who chopped, chopped, and chopped some more.

With each cut another clean slate. I was learning to exhale and to breathe deeply. I even gave her an earful. At the end of my haircut, I had a predictable reaction: I could not recognize myself. They'd given me an A-line layered cut that was shorter in the back than front and angular. They did wonders with the gel, the blow dry, and the iron. But it didn't last. Once I washed it, my curly mane resisted these hair instruments, even after I'd applied gobs of goop. My curly hair unceremoniously sprung up from the sides and top of my head, giving me a symbolic lift I had not even imagined in my wildest dreams. Now I had a puffy, wavy, and sometimes frizzy version of a bob. It turns out my hair is very stubborn! So much so that I've just decided to give in again, let it stage its own little revolú now and then—and break out of the confines of the intended hair-do. I figured something's got to give in these hard times, something's got to support my social and political views (which at times feel lonely). So I take a cue from the hair. The Afro Boricua Latina/o hair talks back, persists, affirms, reaches for the stars, transgresses social limits and is my loving foundation. In some ways, she shows me the power of persistence and the necessity of change. And yet she is generous and wise enough to understand that she possesses a lot of symbolic currency and many incarnations. Meaning, that she can accommodate a variety of hairstyles and is very malleable to a range of new meanings, forms of progressive politics, and self-expression. At times, she goes straight, teams up with dress-up sweat pants and tennis shoes. At times, she is frizzy and teams up with a sweater, a necklace, and a scarf.

Whichever the case, she and I both agree that people should not be judged negatively by how they do their hair. For example, this happened to a Latina presenter who was giving a commencement speech in 2012 at the

University of Arizona and criticized SB 1070 and HB2281. In the middle of her speech, a man screamed out, "Cut Your Hair." Turns out her curly hair bothered him as much as her message.[6] No one should have to submit to this type of hair burden. Neither should we have to force ourselves into one politically correct (hair) response.

Recently, YouTube and television videos aired eye-catching moving pictures of protestors from all over the world, fighting against greed, cultural regulation, downsizing, and lack of access. The protestors showed us that our cultural imaginations are big and wide, braided and straight, curly and frizzy, black and gray, bountiful and, yes, bald! What the moving photos did not tell us about are all of the intriguing and complex ways that hair matters are layered with different social burdens, waves, possibilities, and, yes, stories of affirmation and resistance that speak to the present as well as the future. I can't wait for these hair stories to sprout up and see the light of day. They can help us "reimagine and renegotiate our relationships with other people as well as ourselves,"[7] and just maybe these stories can help us envision a brighter day where we can make peace and chant along with Emily: "I love My Hair."

References

Caldwell, P. M. (2000). A Hair Piece: Perspectives on the Intersection of Race and Gender. In (Eds.) Delgado, R. & Stefancic, J., *Critical Race Theory: The Cutting Edge*, (pp. 275–85). Philadelphia, PA: Temple University Press

Chabram-Dernersesian, A. (2009). Growing Up Mexirican. *Latino Studies*, 7, 378–392.

Kahlo, F. (2012). Self-Portrait with Cropped Hair. Retrieved March 13, 2012, http://www.moma.org/collection/object.php?object_id=7833

Matheson, A. (2011). *I love My Hair*. Oakville, CA: Flowerpots Press.

Mercer, K. (1990). Black Hair/Style Politics. In (Eds.) Ferguson, R., Gever, M., Minh-ha, T. T. & West, C., *Out There: Marginalization and Contemporary Cultures*. New York: The New Museum of Contemporary Art.

Nikki, C. (2012). Manifesto of a Former Self-Hater Blog. Retrieved March 1, 2012. http://questfortheperfectcurl.com/2010/12/03/manifesto-of-a-former-self-hater/

Ochoa, G. (1984). *Becoming Neighbors*. Austin, TX: University of Texas Press.

---

[6]See, Who saw this coming? Latina Professor booed at Arizona graduation for criticizing Arizona, http://guanabee.com/2010/05/sandra-soto-booed-at-graduation/
[7]See George Lipsitz in edited book with Angie Chabram-Dernersesian, *The Chicana/o Cultural Studies Forum*, p. 195.

Owens, T. P. (2002). Hey girl, am I more than my hair? Retrieved March 1, 2012, http://destee.com/index.php?threads/hey-girl-am-i-more-than-my-hair-extended-analysis.45019/.

Taymor, J. (Director). (2002). *Frida*[Motion picture]. Canada: Miramax Films.

_____. (2012). Who Saw This Coming? Latina Professor Booed At Arizona Graduation For Criticizing Arizona. Retrieved March 1, 2012, http://guanabee.com/2010/05/sandra-soto-booed-at-graduation/.

I Grew Up 'Undoing' Colonized Gender

Cindy Cruz

There is a photo of me at four, wearing blue jeans and a sweatshirt, one ponytail missing, with my father and my dog in our backyard. Playing with Tonka trucks, the green water hose making a river run through my construction site, I was happy building roads and bridges. I remember my days filled with play and I wasn't concerned with getting dirty or messy. My mother dressed me in sweatshirts and jeans all through elementary school, tennis shoes or rugged hiking boots added to my look. I was not forced to wear "girl" clothes and my mother often told us how she wanted my sister and I to be strong women, to not take any shit from anyone, particularly boys, teachers, even future husbands, if that's what we chose to do. I was allowed a freedom that other girls did not have, where gender was not forced upon me or any of us in my family. Gender, in my family, was defined much differently. Our biological sex did not equate to our gender, and our gender roles as brown women did not dictate how we moved through the world or who we desired later on in our lives. I grew up in a household where gender was not an issue simply because my mother, as a Chicana, understood that being a woman in a patriarchal culture, particularly the family my mother grew up in, was limiting and sometimes inferiorizing of women[8]. As her daughters, my mother was not going to allow us to have our worlds reduced because we were brown women, and she fought hard to make sure we had every opportunity to live a life much different than her own. Our family had a history of strong women, matriarchs, and

---

[8]Lugones discusses the issues of gender and colonization in her 2008 essay Heterosexualism and the Colonial/Modern Gender System (*Hypatia* 22 (1):186–209), where she states that gender is part of the new social orders imposed on the Americas during the time of colonization. In essence, Lugones is arguing that gender is an introduction, dehumanizing for both women and men and otherly gendered folks, and used to destroy people, cosmologies, and communities.

midwives who lived lives around and for other women. My mother was determined to reclaim our power as women who had once led our family out of Durango, Mexico, by foot during the revolution, and who were powerful as leaders of their communities and families.

I used to think I got my masculinity from my father, but really I learned my butchness from my mother. Tough and unassuming, my mother was critical of the ways she was raised by my grandfather and not allowed to go to college or to join the army like she wanted. In San Gabriel, California, our family in the 1930s and 1940s worked the agricultural fields in the San Gabriel Valley, picked citrus, tilled, watered and fertilized the land in early Los Angeles County. My mother often worked by my grandmother's side making food for the crowd of Mexican farm workers that would break for lunch. At 7, 8, and 9 years old, my mother made tortillas all morning and afternoon as my grandmother cooked, and imagined another life for herself and her sisters and brothers. My grandfather refused my mother the opportunity to go to college, believing that a college education was wasted on women, but he also didn't allow my mother to join the army.[9] My mom considered becoming a nun, anything that would offer her a certain amount of autonomy as a young Chicana in the late 1950s, taking live-in nanny jobs for rich white families in Hollywood and Toluca Lake. My mother worked hard and when she met my father, a handsome man who was already a union steelworker, she was ready to marry him.

One thing about my parent's relationship—it was a partnership where gender roles were not fixed and ridged. My sister and brother and I grew up in a household where we talked to each other, we heard our parents talk early in the morning over coffee. We have dozens of family albums in our home, documenting our family's life in Los Angeles and in Fontana, and I never tired of browsing through them. Only recently, though, in an iconic portrait of my mother and father sitting at La Golondrina Restaurant in downtown Los Angeles before they were married, did I notice in my mother's firm hand the word "lovers" handwritten across the bottom of the photograph. Desire and love existed between my parents despite patriarchy, the job ceiling and often dangerous work my father did, and the segregation of Mexican families in Fontana. It wasn't until I met the families of my friends and neighbors where I learned that some families were organized in much different ways, where gender was prominent, and the rules to what a young woman or man should be were much different and often oppressive.

---

[9]My grandmother, a mother of 11 children and a devoted Catholic, divorced my grandfather in 1953, when it was very rare for any women to file for divorce.

One of the things that I did growing up in Fontana was that I chose to go to church. Little church buses would come to my neighborhood in the summertime and pick up children for bible study and sermon. Church folks would recruit us by offering cake and punch or new bibles, or even money to attend their churches. Bored during the hot summers, my friends and I boarded those buses into local Methodist, Episcopalian, and Baptist churches, and I usually was the only brown girl sitting in the pews. But I liked bible study because it was like school, and I enjoyed reading about the stories of the Old Testament and learning with the use of song for every chapter of the bible, "Genesis, Exodus, Leviticus, Numbers . . ." I was the best student in bible class, and relished the attention I got from the teachers. One bible camp in particular had a talented teacher and I was in her class. The reverend of the church asked the teacher to tell me that I needed to wear a dress to Sunday school, and I said no. I didn't own a dress and I wasn't about to wear one. This infuriated the reverend, as the church was changing and more and more girls whose families were congregants began to wear long dresses to the ankle and cover their arms, despite the heat. Girls bore the brunt of whatever gender changes were happening to this church, and with my short haircut and jeans and t-shirts, I was asked not to come back to the church. I was 12 years old.

What was it about my short hair and boots and jeans that were so threatening to this reverend and his church? I remember leaving the church in the middle of a sermon and seeing my teacher running toward me from the Sunday school offices to catch me as I walked home. She wanted to let me know that I did not need to let this incident affect my faith. I knew then that my existence had offended this reverend by transgressing my gender role—he sometimes looked so incredulous when I walked by him during bible study—and I had trespassed long enough. But I was not shaken, and I knew it was the reverend's inability to see me as a viable part of the church community. But I also sensed that this was going to be the beginning of other people's reactions to my otherly gendered body, as I began to not be seen as a "tomboy," but rather now as a "queer." Somewhere, somehow my gender transgressions had upset the social organization of this church community, and to have a queer child in this colonial institution threatened the rules and regulations of how women and men could be with each other. I had outgrown the "pass" I was afforded as a child and now as an adolescent, the policing of gender became almost unbearable as peers, parents, teachers, even doctors commented harshly on my clothes, my walk, their inability to tell whether I was a man or a woman.

I think about this experience now as a queer academic, where my work centers the stories and testimonios of LGBTQ youth, who have similar histories of trespassing and transgression in different spaces and places in their own lives. Gender in my home was fluid and open and the partnership my parents shared—as a collaborative and nonhierarchical trust—was my model for relating differently with other people. If gender is this thing that is imposed onto the inhabitants of the New World as part of reorganizing how conquerors saw the Native as less than human, then when families reject traditional gender systems for both men and women, that is a radical thing. You learn to say "no" to domination, to resist these colonizing ways. In my family, I learned that decolonization begins with "undo-ing" gender, and I thank my mother and my father in allowing us to reject the model many times offered to us under domination since the 1500s.

Boricua and College Educated

Rebecca Rosa

My mother came to the mainland from Puerto Rico when she was twelve; the year was 1954. There were no bilingual or ELD (English Language Development) classes and she was forced to learn English. Ingrained from the moment she entered the Russian Hill/Marina District classroom, she quickly learned; speaking her primary language, her only language, was not tolerated. In the 1950s, corporal punishment was commonplace and its use was not banned in California until 1987. Subsequently, my mother was afraid to speak Spanish at school. She learned to read, write, and speak English within three months. The message was clear, assimilate and your teachers will not beat you. The acculturation process had taken hold. She ate hot dogs and hamburgers for lunch. She dressed like her peers, acted like her peers, and adopted many of their behaviors and values.

My father, who is 100 percent Puerto Rican, was born in Hawaii and is one of thirteen children. My grandmother's parents left Puerto Rico to work in the sugar cane fields on the island of Hawaii where my grandmother was born on the Hilo side. My paternal grandfather was a longshoreman born in Puerto Rico and he met and married my grandmother in Hawaii. They moved to the mainland when my father was six. My grandparents did not teach any of their thirteen children their primary language. They only spoke English at home.

My parents met in high school and married after graduation. By the time I was four, they moved out of the city and bought a house in a white neighborhood. They were fulfilling what they deemed as "The American Dream."

I attended parochial school and was surrounded by a predominantly European American community. In fact, in a class of thirty students who traveled from first to eighth grade together, I was one of three Latino children and the only Puerto Rican. Both my parents worked and my maternal grandmother took care of me after school. My grandmother lived in California for over fifty years and did not speak a word of English. She shopped in the Mission District, spoke only Spanish, and watched her novellas on the television. She held on. I learned to speak Spanish because of her. The little I learned about my Puerto Rican culture came predominantly from her, through her stories, her memories, and her food. I loved when she recited the folktales about *Juan Bobo*.

At school, there was no one like me. I can count on one hand the number of times Puerto Rico was mentioned in my classes throughout my K-12 education. In the primary grades, Christopher Columbus was hailed a hero. I learned the traditional narrative, the one-dimensional glorification of "a courageous explorer who discovered America." In high school, Puerto Rico was portrayed as a colony of the United States that "enjoyed" many benefits and privileges under the "protection" of the United States. As James Loewen wrote, I learned the "lies my teacher told me."

Every few years, my paternal family gets together at a community park in the East Bay for a family reunion. Generally held during the month of July, we all pitch our party tents, unfold our camp chairs, and turn up the salsa and merengue. As a child, the family reunions were an opportunity for me to eat the delicacies of the island, lechon (roast pork), arroz con gandules, pasteles, alcapurrias, and platanos. It was a time to catch up with family members and to play with my cousins; I have thirty-three first cousins alone. As the years went by, I noticed during family gatherings my older cousins sporting T-shirts with the word "Boricua" over the Puerto Rican flag. My nuclear family had become so acculturated I had to ask my mother, "What is a Boricua?" It was the first time I heard of the Taínos, the Native people of Puerto Rico. The term "Boricua" goes back centuries and can be found in books and poems over 200 years old. Boricua comes from the Taíno word for the island, Boriken, meaning valiant people. Boricua and Puerto Rican are used interchangeably. The island's national anthem is La Borinqueña.

The damage done by decades of acculturation had taken its toll on my identity and I wanted to reclaim my heritage. I needed to learn more, more about my mother, my father, my roots, and me. I embarked on a journey to learn more about my history. My grandfather was born in Aguadilla, Puerto Rico. Located just five miles from Aguada, the city known as *La Ciudad Del Descubrimiento*, as it is believed that Columbus landed in Aguada in November of 1493. Why hadn't anyone shared this with me? Upon entering college, I took a history course where I learned about colonialization, imperialism, and the realities of Columbus' in the Caribbean. I was horrified and angry! Why wasn't I exposed to the untold stories? Why didn't I know about the rich history, struggle and survival of my people? What other misinformation had I been fed throughout my formal education?

In the midst of my anger, I found my calling. I knew I wanted to teach adolescents, I wanted to be the social studies teacher who pushed back against the traditional narrative; the teacher who taught multiple perspectives; the teacher who gave her students a broader, more comprehensive, inclusive view of history. I needed to be the teacher who taught her students to engage in critical thought, to question, and to participate in critical discourse; the teacher who encouraged students to learn about and embrace their cultural heritage and background. In the midst of my anger, I found myself.

From the island's Native People, to the European colonizers, to the African slaves, Puerto Ricans are an amalgamation of different cultural groups who lived on the island throughout its history. I am the only cousin who is 100 percent Puerto Rican. When I think about it, being 100 percent from any cultural background is rare. I lovingly refer to my family as the United Nations. We have Mexican-Puerto Ricans, German-Puerto Ricans, Japanese-Puerto Ricans, Samoan-Puerto Ricans, French-Puerto-Ricans, African American-Puerto Ricans, Filipino-Puerto Ricans and Russian-Puerto Ricans. Yet, we all come together every other year to celebrate family, to learn more about our heritage, and to take pride in that we are Puerto Ricans. Last April, my family decided to hold the family reunion at the Festival de la Isla (Puerto Rican Festival). I proudly wore a shirt with a Puerto Rican flag and the phrase, "¡Oye, soy Boricua pa que tú lo sepas!" I am Boricua just so you know.

From the Andes to College Town USA: Life Affirmations across Generations of Amerindian Women

Sofia Villenas

It is incredible to think about the journeys of women across time and space—from South America to North America, from childhoods experienced in the 1940s to the 1970s and 1990s, from generational poverty to a middle class professional household, from Spanish to English to Spanglish and back again. These are threads of tradition and change. Like a palimpsest, erased and overwritten, traces of what was there before reappear to animate our lives over generations. What reappear in our stories are the injuries of racism, gender, poverty and class, alongside *rebeldias* (rebellions), aspirations, and life affirmations.

I am a second-generation child of immigrant parents from Ecuador. I am the daughter of my mother, Hilda, who grew up in poverty in a rural town called Pomasqui located just north of downtown Quito, Ecuador's capital city. In my mother's stories, she describes some of the hardships of her childhood:

> *No teníamos zapatos para ir a la escuela, solamente los domingos nos poníamos los zapatos. Y nuestra comida era pura colada, con harina de maíz, con caldo, y sólo los domingos hacía el arroz. Para mí el arroz era como comida de ricos, y el huevo frito también. Leche no tomábamos.*

> *We didn't have shoes to go to school, only on Sundays did we wear shoes. And our food was just colada (porridge) with corn flour, with broth, and only on Sundays did I make rice. For me, rice was like the food of the rich, and fried egg too. Milk, we didn't drink.*

My grandmother, Mamita Hortencia, died when my mother was only nine years old. My grandfather, Papá Esperidion, who grew corn, beans, and potatoes for a living, did the best he could to raise my mother and her siblings. My mother describes what it was like to grow up without Mamita, and the hard work that fell upon her and her younger sister, my aunt Sylvia:

> *Por que vés que Papá todos los días iba al terreno en la mañanita y venía en la tarde y nosotros pasábamos solitas todo el día . . . y el trabajo más difícil era que teníamos que cocinar, poner leña . . . y teníamos que rapido hacer comida para regresar a la escuela . . . y no teníamos reloj, teníamos que ver el sol en la pared que baje.*

> *Because see Papá everyday went to the fields in the early morning and returned in the late afternoon, and we were alone all day . . . and the most difficult work was that we had to cook, get the fire going . . . and we had to quickly make the food so we could go back to school . . . and we didn't have a clock, we had to watch the sun on the wall go down.*

I asked my mother "Who taught you things and who guided you?" She answered emphatically, "Nadie mija, nadie, nadie, nadie" (no one my daughter, no one, no one, no one). Papá's sadness at Mamita's passing and his long hours in the fields often meant a lack of affection and *consejos* (advice) for his daughters:

> *En ese tiempo no teníamos televisión y no habían programas así como ahora mucho hablan de los padres con los hijos, y los hijos para con los padres. O sea nos criamos sin amor. Papá nunca era aparente para darnos un abrazo, decirnos te quiero, les quiero, No, y nosotros nos criamos de esa manera, y por eso yo también me creí con ustedes así. Yo nunca les decía te quiero, no como ahora, a los nietos, les digo te*

quiero mucho. Si nosotros fuimos frías es por que no teníamos cariño de los padres y nadie nos enseñó . . . sin tener un consejo de mama.

In those days, we didn't have television and there weren't programs like today about parents talking with their kids and kids with their parents. In other words, we grew up without love. Papá wasn't into giving us a hug, or telling us "I love you." No, and we grew up that way, and that's why I also raised you [you and your brothers] that way, I would never tell you I loved you, not like now with the grandchildren, I tell them "I love you very much." If we were cold it was because we didn't have a parent's affection and nobody taught us . . . we didn't have the advice of a mother.

My mother goes on to tell me about how as teenagers, she and her siblings were loved in the community, especially by their peers. She and her sister Sylvia were especially popular. They were good kids and had good values. But expectations for women were limited to home and housewife. My mother says, "*Yo me desesperaba por trabajar*" (I was desperate to work). She wanted to supplement the family income and to buy clothes so that she and her sister might be better dressed. But Papá would not let her work and in her *rebeldia*, she would sneak out to go job hunting in Quito.

My mother had aspirations of coming to the United States. Her older brother was already here, and he eventually called for Papá and his unmarried daughters to join him. My mother says, "*Yo sí que me desesperaba para salir del Ecuador. Decía, 'yo quiero salir, no sé a donde pero yo QUIERO salir de aquí de Quito, o de Pomasqui'*" (I was desperate to get out of Ecuador. I would say, "I want to leave, I don't know where to but I WANT to get out of Quito, or from Pomasqui.") My mother did leave and as she tells it, immediately liked the United States, with new hardships and all.

Recently, I visited my mother in her apartment in Southern California. I enjoy and appreciate how she affirms her life in so many ways. I admired the great care she took in making her home a beautiful sanctuary. I admired the great respect she had for herself in taking care of her nutrition, her body with daily exercise and yoga, and her skin and hair. Her life came into focus for me. I remembered her fortitude and resilience in maneuvering the labyrinth of California institutions as a predominantly Spanish speaker. I remembered her life as a learner in adult English-as-a-second language and vocational classes. I admired how hard she always worked in and out of the home and her amazing frugalness with a working class household income. Now, I am reminded of my own upbringing. I grew up enjoying material comforts that she never did. Yet for the children of the Latino diaspora, there are new experiences that are difficult to communicate. For example, I didn't have the words to express what it felt like to be racialized and minoritized in U.S. schools as a brown, Spanish-speaking "Latin person." I didn't see myself or other Latinas/os, not even Mexican Americans, included in the curriculum. I didn't see our bilingual lives represented in the books we read. How could I communicate this isolation and exclusion? How could I communicate the burden I felt in my responsibilities as a child translator, or express the joy I felt in living and breathing Ecuador through my parents' stories and the letters from my *tias* (aunts) and *primas* (woman cousins)? And like her father, my mother did not tell me she loved me, and rarely gave me a hug, though I knew she loved us dearly.

My own 18-year-old daughter, Atzín, has grown up these last seven years in Ithaca, a college town in central New York. I tell her she is lucky she does not have to translate for me as I did for my mother. She also does not qualify for free and reduced lunch because her Ph.D. mamá receives a professional salary. And unlike my experience at her age, she has the tools to communicate the dissonance she experiences when she does not see Latino history in the curriculum, or when she is racialized and stereotyped, or when she is faced with distorted gendered messages from peers and the media about how to dress and behave. She reads Chicana literature, with Helena Viramontes's *The Dogs Came with Them* being among her favorites. Though she may not experience it as such, I want her to know that she is following in the spirit of a long line of Amerindian women. One day two years ago, Atzin asked with tears in her eyes, "Why don't you ever hug me?"

Entre mis Llantos Encuentro mi Espíritu

Margarita I. Berta-Avila

As a single parent, my mother worked hard to make sure I did not go without the essentials. She promoted "education" as a pathway to future success and endeavors. My mother sacrificed monetarily and enrolled me in a Catholic parochial school. In order to do so, every dollar was accounted for. Simply put, each check was budgeted to pay for food, the rent, and bills. No frivolous spending was ever made. She would save throughout the year (approximately a total of $100.00) to be able to buy what I needed for school like my uniforms and books. All of these sacrifices were made with the belief that I would receive a quality education in a private institution. Because my mother instilled in me feelings of hope, possibilities, and excitement that come with attending school, I entered the first grade ready to excel.

Three weeks into my first grade year, my teacher handed me an enclosed envelope to deliver to my mother. Scared out of my mind, I handed over the letter, to find out that my teacher wanted to have a meeting. About what, I had no idea. Several days later, my mother came home late (from meeting with my teacher). I was already in bed. She approached me slowly and as she came closer, I could see the tears swelling up in her eyes. It was at that moment when she was about to give life to her words that I could feel my fear take over me. She sat down and stated "Marguita, the teacher told me that if I did not stop speaking Spanish to you she would fail you from the first grade." From that day forward, my mother no longer spoke to me in our native tongue. Though at six years old, I could not name what was happening . . . the message I clearly received was that to succeed I had to abandon me . . . without directly stating it . . . I had to abandon my *Spirit*.

To this day, I still cannot express in words the pain that single act caused. I recall easily succumbing to the messages posed by school, the mass media, and the community at large. I was convinced that my Raza community had less value than its White counterpart. This led me to being ashamed of my mother's Salvadorian and my father's Peruvian cultural heritage. Ultimately, I came to see them both as inferior. Even though I was quite aware of everything my mother had sacrificed. It didn't matter. I had turned to drinking, began to experiment with drugs, and quite often put myself in dangerous situations that should have landed me dead. Though I didn't realize it at that time in my life, it's evident to me now that I was determined to destroy my life. And yet, simultaneously I so desperately wanted to be accepted in the dominant White culture that I was willing to assimilate which led to the silence of my *Voice*, and the death of my *Spirit*.

At the age of sixteen, my mother felt the best thing for me was to leave the States and visit my family in Peru (South America). I was spiraling out of control and I had left her no choice. During this particular trip, my Tía Lili (aunt) who was very much involved with issues of social justice decided to act as my cultural broker (Darder, 1991) and spoke to me seriously about the inhumane treatment of Native people and their lands, exploitation of children, abusive conditions of workers, inadequate health care for the poor, inequitable access to education, and so on. As she spoke to me, I remember distinctly taking it all in, absorbing the information she was sharing with me, but not knowing really what I was supposed to do with it . . . until I reached Machu Pichu, "Old Peak," a significant site that was never conquered by the Spaniards but abandoned by the Incas as a result of the Spanish conquest/invasion.

Initially, like any young teenager, I approached our visit to Machu Pichu as a tourist attraction. We woke up early in the morning to catch the train because that was the only way you could obtain access. As the Sun rose from the east, for miles and miles, all I could see were fields and the gente (people) beginning to wake up to cultivate the land. As the train made its way through El Valle Sagrado (The Sacred Valley), I felt something in me stirring as if I knew this place, as if I knew this land, as if I had been here before . . . but I just tried to brush it off—dismissing my feelings. We finally reached the base of Machu Pichu where we boarded a bus. Slowly, we zig-zagged our way up the mountain. With every zig and every zag, we were further distancing ourselves from all the people, all the noise, and all the bullshit (at least for me). A sense of serenity was overtaking me and this time I didn't try to ignore it . . . I allowed it in because I felt I was somehow coming home.

As we approached the entrance I was so nervous—my whole demeanor in a matter of hours had changed from one of a tourist frame of mind to one of humility. We got off the bus and followed the crowd toward a small door. We didn't reach this door right away as people were taking their time to enter—little by little we got closer until my Tía turned to me and stated "Estas lista? Are you ready?" We opened the door together and before me was the most spectacular site I had ever seen. A majestic city cradled between two powerful mountains, Machu Pichu and Huayna Pichu. Outside the perimeters of this cradle, one could look down and take in the beautiful site of two valleys. More importantly, it did not matter which direction you turned, the city reflected what was important to the community that lived in this space: sanctuaries, residences, parks, and temples. To walk around and take note of the phenomenal architecture, you had to follow the hundreds of stone steps the Incas carved from blocks of granite. There was so much to take in that all I could do was gasp. As I inhaled to take those breathes in, tears rolled down my eyes. I couldn't explain it. I couldn't understand it and my Tía just nodded to me in acknowledgment. Without saying anything, her affirmation of my tears gave me the permission to begin the process of calling back my *Spirit*.

Slowly, we walked and visited every aspect of Machu Pichu as we listened to the guide explain the history of this spectacular ancestral site. But something was calling me to keep walking further up . . . it was almost a feeling of urgency to reach the top. I asked my Tía—if we could leave the group and go to the top. I walked as fast as I could. Once we reached what I felt was my final destination, in front of me was "El Observatorio Astrónomico del Intihuatana," one of the most sacred places in Machu Pichu—the Sun Stone. As I stood in front of this sacred space, my Tía whispered in my ear that many believe this particular site is the most spiritual of all and that if you allow yourself you can feel our ancestral spirits and the messages they have for us.

As my Tía finished sharing, I walked toward the edge of the mountain. I could see all of Machu Pichu. Without really knowing what I was doing, I closed my eyes and held out the palms of my hands to face the Sun. I began to pray. For me—this was the turning point. A decision was upon me—to continue on the path I was on . . . of utter destruction or I could reclaim my life. Suddenly, waves of energy moved up and down my body. Though my eyes were closed, I could sense that everything around me was gray and that I was alone. Then I heard their voices. From the depths of my BODY, my ancestors—my grandmothers my grandfathers—called out to me . . . called out to my Spirit to fully come back. To come back because the work that lay ahead of me was too important—my responsibility was to dedicate my life to obtain justice for our people. Thus, there was no choice to make. Why? Because I am a part of them as they are a part of me. Therefore, no doubt should exist about who I am and where I am from. Because I am this land I embody this earth—and no one can ever take that away.

Just as quickly as that experience came to me, it ended. I opened my eyes trying to figure out if anybody else had experienced the same thing. The only person that appeared to be paying attention to me was this young man a few feet away from me. As I looked at him, he smiled. He walked over to me and shared that I should not take for granted this gift that was given to me. Heed the message and move forward always grounded in Spirit. He offered one last smile and walked away. Stunned by everything I found my Tía who said, "Encontrastes lo que estabas buscando?/Did you find what you were looking for?" "Sí, Tía/ Yes, Tia." "Muy bien/Very good."

When I came back to the States, I immediately became aware of things I had not noticed before but that had always existed. Inequities and injustices had now become apparent to me and I suddenly found myself asking "Why? Why did I not see this before? Why are we not talking about this in school? Why are we not being told the truth?" It was in this process of asking questions that my Tia's teachings and my experience in Machu Pichu became clear: Even if the experiences of others appear to not have an effect on us, they do. We have a responsibility to one another, a responsibility to help each other achieve internal/external liberation. A responsibility to work for equity and justice for all marginalized people, based on race, class, gender, language, sexual orientation, and other differences. Whether this experience was an epiphany or a veil covering my eyes, that was finally lifted (Freire, 1970), I knew I could no longer look at our world or my role in it the same. My *Spirit* had come back and there was much to do.

References

Darder, A. (1991). *Culture and power in the classroom: A critical foundation for bicultural education.* Westport, CT: Bergin & Garvey.

Freire, P. (1970). *Pedagogy of the oppressed.* New York, NY: Seabury Press.

Dreams and Transitions: Connecting My Past in My Present

Caroline Sotello Viernes Turner

I know that I am connected to my ancestors and their legacy even though I never met my grandparents on either my mother's or my father's side. I have experienced this invisible, real connection when I am in the midst of highly stressful, wrenching transitions.

As a daughter of a farm worker family, I left everything I knew to go to college. When I finished my doctorate, I was facing another major change. With my daughter and son, I was getting ready to accept my first faculty position out of state. I was leaving my mother, my sisters, my brother, and my home state.

It is during this latter transition that the thread of my past connected to my present, opening windows to self-understanding and providing me with the courage to move on. I have had three powerful dream experiences in my life when a curandera appears to provide an insight into my situation. I want to share one with you here.

My Dream

I was in a cage. I felt trapped. I was all movement, trying to break free of this confining place. Then I realized I had hooves and a sleek brown body. I was so nervous and my mind was racing ahead. I wanted to get out of the cage. I could hear a voice trying to calm me down. Actually, it was my own voice, telling me to calm down; otherwise I would not get a good start out of the gate. I was a race horse poised to start a race. I knew that I needed a good start in order to win this race. It was odd that I was a horse. I am really afraid of horses. They are so big. Yet, I admire their strength and power. I never took any interest in horse racing so when I awoke from this dream, I couldn't imagine where the feelings and visions I was having as the horse in a cage came from.

The gate opened and the starting bell rang. I could feel the wind against my face and in my hair, the dirt under my hooves. I did not look to the side or back. I only looked forward and with the strong but graceful movements of a seasoned runner headed for the finish line. I realized that I was high strung and vulnerable, however. My legs, while strong, were thin for my frame and if they were injured I would be of little use on a race track. The finish line was straight ahead, I could feel no rival by my side.

As I reached the finish line, I turned into a white-winged horse. I flew up into the sky where I could get a panoramic view of the track I just ran, but now my wings held me above the ground. I felt victorious and strong. My body was fuller and stronger but in a different way. Not the way of the nervous and fragile race horse, but the way of strength that came from a heavier body and limbs made to fly over the earth. That was strange too because to fly you would think that being lighter would be better.

While I viewed the track below me, I came to realize that life may be made up of these anxious moments as you encounter life's transitions, then as the challenge is met you fly over the landscape thinking that you will never travel there again and be that nervous and vulnerable again, but that's not true.

Races such as these, at different planes as in a spiral of one's life, will be run over and over again. There will always be new beginnings and transitions to be encountered and overcome, and the feeling of flying afterward, but these experiences are all part of a never ending cycle of being vulnerable and being victorious. Somehow just knowing this helps me to address life changes and transitions as well as the challenges posed during these times.

Reflections on the Curandera and Dreams

Belief in a curandera and the existence of spirit visits emerges from my Native Mexican and Philipino roots. A curandera is a healer, a therapist. In my dreams, she is wearing a black cloak with a hood and asks that I not look at her but keep my back to her as she brings visions to me. This requires trust on my part and faith that she exists even if I cannot directly face her. Growing up on farm labor camps, I heard stories about the existence of a curandera among the laborers living in the corrugated steel shacks we inhabited. The curandera was always described as a woman with powers to heal; she is part of the peoples from which we are descendants. She is part of our collective legacy. I remember families leaving the labor camp and taking their ailing relative to be cured by a curandera. I always felt that I was part of this tradition even though my parents did not take their ailing relatives to a curandera.

I feel that the horse, the track, and the cage are connected to my Native roots by providing a path for conscious insight from a curandera through dreams (the spiritual experience) into my present. The horse is a powerful animal grounded on earth and also belonging to the air. I can be strong in both places of being. The track represents a restricted place where the horse is compelled to run when released from the confines of a cage while the winged horse is liberated and has endless possibilities in reach. I can be both the race horse and the winged horse. The transformation to a flying horse is made possible when the race around the track finds you triumphant and rising above life's challenges. This is possible through the support of those who are connected to us in the past and in the present.

Now, because of my own dream experiences, I believe that this power of insight exists and is always with me. It comes from those who lived before me, who are a part of me as I am a part of them. I cannot control when the curandera's insight comes to me but it is connected to my past and manifests itself in my present. I can feel, hear, and see these dreams so vividly. They are intense and life-like. They come when I need them. I also believe that I would not have these experiences without a belief in possibilities beyond what I was taught to expect. My learning to date has opened my mind to understand that there are endless possibilities in terms of ways of knowing. Dreaming is as important to my life's journey as any other way of knowing. It connects my past in my present. In dreaming, I know that my past is a part of me always, forever connected to my present.

A Testimony of Healing in Nuevo México, Aztlan

Ruth Trinidad-Galván

Farmington

Only 20 miles after entering the state of Nuevo Mexico, 3 daughters in tote and a truck full of luggage, healing seria la bienvenida. The next 500 miles to our new home did not initially rest on the place's potential to heal or predict the traumas that would impact my life for the next few years—but indeed it did.

On that day, the pains that were beginning to surge through my female brown body were the reason for our first initial stop in that small northern city of Farmington. I might have been clueless to the discomfort after half of day of mindless and numbing driving from Salt Lake City to leave my graduate program for my first academic position, but just 2 days prior, my gynecologist had informed me that we were expecting our fourth child. Although my womb was fertile, the relationship was not—so it pained me on many levels as I cried uncontrollably in my midwife's office on the day that I was given the news. I had actually visited her office with the intention of receiving preventive methods as we prepared to take the voyage and start "hopefully" a new life on new soil. Although it felt like every move since leaving our native Los Angeles seemed to signal a "new" life—the move to Salt Lake City then to Central Mexico and then back to Salt Lake City—the moves had somehow fallen short of that outcome. And yet, here we were, driving to a new place with three wonderful daughters and hopes again for a "new" beginning.

I tried to ignore the pain and move on—I wanted to arrive to our new home, to our new beginnings, to new held possibilities. Our arrival to Albuquerque, Nuevo México, took us straight to the first hospital we found—down Route 66—to Presbyterian Hospital. Indeed, I had likely miscarried, but they wouldn't be sure until the next day when they could check with certainty my HCG levels. I would learn later that he would blame me for the loss even though the doctors clearly stated there was nothing that could have prevented the outcome. In agony, I wrote my first words of healing in Nuevo México on the anniversary of the event:

> No hay mal, que por bien no venga
>
> eso suelen decir
>
> Pero como es que – no te desee, ni te espere,
>
> pero todavía así te extrañe
>
> La lección quizás fue tierna,
>
> pero de ninguna manera justa

Chaco Canyon

Indeed my first words of healing in Nuevo México would not heal me of the biggest disillusionment—a marriage that ended. Guilt engrossed me to no end years leading to and after the failing end, and so once again, I tried to heal in various ways.

I decided to visit the grand land of Chaco Canyon alone. My girls were spending the summer with their father. Of course, it meant that I'd waited until the hottest month of the year—July—to visit. I went to heal the wounds of a very civil but emotionally wearing divorce. I was intent on embracing this land for its healing potential—a ceremonial nucleus and spiritual place.

The drive was just over two hours northwest of my home in Albuquerque and off the main road. On that day, there were few visitors and interestingly enough mostly campers. Although the sun was hot and, like most days in Nuevo México, very dry it felt good to be surrounded by the antiquity and history of the place. As I walked and explored those old structures full of history and collective memory, I reflected on the almost two years that had transpired, so much destruction and dolor. And yet here I was surrounded by history and silence. The lesson was simple, in the larger scope of things; the place made emotions of the here and now seem small and petty. It didn't minimize my feelings—I understood them as real—yet its longstanding history, the lives that had set foot on this land, and their eventual departure meant all peoples, all emotions, all feelings, all actions come, move on and dissipate. And so I took that lesson—el tiempo y el cambio siempre te lleva a la sanación.

In lots of ways in Chaco Canyon, I was reminded and saw the connections to the Native ceremonial spaces of Teotihuacan and Templo Mayor in Mexico

City, Palenque in Chiapas, and Chichen Itza in Yucatan, all places I knew so well. The sacred structures and tranquility of these spaces and places made it easy to search within and be reminded of self in connection to others, to places, and to the significance of human change. I imaged the changes that my ancestors, particularly the women of these places, must have encountered after the pre-Colombian era. My search and visits to these Native spaces and places of reflection taught me to leave those feelings and emotions on paper. And so, as I represented in my journal, I came undone in order to acknowledge life, death and rebirth, as well as detach, perdonar y olvidar.

Visual Journal: "She's Come Undone" by Ruth Trinidad-Galván

Albuquerque

My body betrays me

Me rechaza, me condena

Yet I need it to remain complete

My healing was different in 2004, when I was diagnosed with breast cancer and tried to manage the disease as best I could. At the time, it all seemed tireless and endless. Not only did it feel like my body betrayed me, but also that it turned me into someone else—body and spirit. Illnesses are often depicted as life-changing moments in which we glean a brand new "meaning of life". Indeed this might be so and to some extent fue así para mi también. For me, the "meaning of life" was secondary to the immediacy of attending to a journey in which I might lose myself. Lose not my desire and passion for life—for how can that be lost in the face of death. Si no mas bien pederme en las cicatrices de la angustia y el temor.

And in the process, I had to appear normal, joyful of life, llena de vida—especially in the eyes of those that relied on me most—my daughters. As I look back at my journal entries of that time, I realize how much effort it required to not curse the world and everyone in it. How important it was to express that anger on paper and how lonely the process was even in the company of so many wonderful friends and loved ones.

Healing at the time was a mode of survival of the immediate type—at times soul searching, always grateful to have the next day, but mostly attentive to the next medical treatment that contributed to that loss of self. How do you remain attentive to an ailing body and simultaneously nourish the soul? It was almost impossible, yet necessary so as not to lose myself in the process.

I found a healing home in Albuquerque, Nuevo México, and an extended familia that were absolutely essential in my own supervivencia. And so, while healing occurred in companionship, I learned that it also had to occur in moments of isolation. All the while, I had consistently said that healing was only possible in convivencia, I came to learn that sometimes that is not possible or wanted during times of ill health. And so in solitude, I also had to find creative ways of healing.

I was reminded, while revisiting the healing from that time ago, that my healing in Nuevo México rested on my ability to find the space, the place, and the medium to shed emotions and create new ones.

Liberación . . .

De los sentimientos y de los dolores

De los amores y de los errores

De los fracasos y de los rechazos

Para poder

Envolverme . . .

De amor y calor

De emoción y afirmación

De vida y duración

Rhythmic Hope: Documenting my Dream to Belong

Marcela S. Jáuregui

A familiar feeling surfaces as I stand waiting to join the revelers in the center. I anxiously listen to their clapping, stomping, snapping, and voices—waiting and hoping to add to their rhythms.

I am a participant of the "rhythm exercise" at the UC Davis Chicana/o Latina/o Leadership Retreat. The activity leader has divided us into our home-groups and given us each a rhythm. He has then chosen people at random from each team – even one whole, lucky home-group – to sound their rhythms in the center of the room, leaving the rest of us in the periphery as spectators to the joyous cacophony of sounds within. Nevertheless, there is hope for us too, since the activity leader continues to walk around the room hand-picking some of us left on the outside to join the center.

I struggle to make eye-contact with the activity leader or "decider" while simultaneously, perhaps subconsciously, trying to seem as innocuous and desirable as possible—meek yet purposeful. My eyes implore: "Choose me. Don't overlook me. Legitimize my presence. Don't keep me on the outside looking in." Our eyes meet and I get the signal—I am part of the fold! I am welcomed to the center and am overjoyed with a sense of belonging.

Yet, despite being in the center, I feel a kindred connection with those still on the outside. I feel fortunate but powerless to help those still looking in, clamoring to be chosen. It is startling that as an actor, on the inside, I feel as powerless as I did on the outside.

Then it hit me: the realization that I see my marginalization as an indocumentada, undocumented Latina immigrant, *displayed before me. The familiar feeling I felt earlier is the same hopefulness coupled with frustration and fear that I confront each day as I face limitations that constrain my personal agency and independence—the inability to work a "regular" job due to my lack of proper documentation, the inability to drive because I have no driver's license, and the quarterly scramble each time tuition is due because I do not have access to Financial Aid or most scholarships to help me finance my educational aspirations.*

I was three-months-old when my parents brought me to the United States. Although I was not fully aware of my status until my senior year of high school, growing up, there always was a sense of otherness. In particular, I recall being told when I was in elementary school never to share details of my Mexican birth to anyone because if I did something bad could happen to my family. The feeling that I could not be wholly me for fear of hurting my family left me disempowered and fractured.

It is heartbreaking to confront the reality that I am considered "alien" to the only land I have ever called home, the United States, simply due to the lack of "papers:" a green card or a visa. In my daily life, I overcompensate with my appearance—in speech, dress, and mannerisms—to try to blend in and appear as "American" as possible, to belong. However, it feels like a losing battle when my whole sense of being and belonging is delegitimized—I am illegal, thrust in the shadows, the scapegoat, and deportable. Being undocumented can be isolating and alienating because, in the end, it is difficult to trust others with my status, for fear of reprisal or rejection. Now, even after I have found my voice and the bravery to disclose my status and origins with pride, the fear persists.

As I stand in the center of the room, in the middle of the action, the fear permeates and colors my experience but in spite of it, I see hope. Hope is represented by those individuals in the middle who go back to their home-group, to give fellow members a connection to the center even as they remain on the outside. Hope is the individuals reminding the "decider" of those forgotten on the periphery. Hope is the individuals on the outside that courageously join the center without "permission."

For me, hope comes in the form of high school teachers and administrators who find a pathway to college for their undocumented students. Hope is my family who gives me the guidance, support, and latitude to follow my educational aspirations far from home. Hope is fellow Dreamers who give me the strength and conviction to move forward—even if we do not have documents, we can still achieve a semblance of the Dream our parents' journey to the United States promised. Hope is the scholarship and mentorship of professors that inspire Dreamers to achieve our educational aims. Hope is the activism of community members who advance the need for comprehensive immigration reform. Hope is my partner, my strongest ally, the one person who motivates and foments my fortitude with his love, encouragement, and advocacy.

As I join my group in our rhythm, I am determined that I, too, can help spread hope—just like all the allies that help me combat the limiting fear and frustration sown by my own undocumented status. I seek to be an ally to give hope and voice to those still seeking to legitimize their presence, to overcome their despair, and to belong.

In closing, my life as an indocumentada is not a monolithic representation of other undocumented immigrants, despite sharing similarities, and is firmly situated in the context of my own particular experience. I am still struggling to come to terms with my status: what it means to me, and how I wish to identify. For me, to be undocumented was not an initial choice, but it is my most distinguishing characteristic, the trait that defines all other aspects of my life and being.

My undocumented status leaves me in a constant state of limbo that situates me precariously in Anzaldúa's Borderlands—ni de aquí, ni de allá. My connections to both American and Mexican cultures are tenuous at best and I will never fully belong to either. Even though my status precludes membership as either an Americana or Mexicana, I hope to maintain a connection with both cultures—my native, Spanish tongue and costumbres as well as those of my adopted country, the only place I have ever known as home—to feel a sense of wholeness and belonging.

My ultimate dream, however, is for comprehensive immigration reform that can bring all undocumented out-of-the-shadows in the United States. My hope is for an end to the limbo that limits our potential and the fear that permeates our lives. My hope is for the legitimization of our presence and the self-determination to construct our own futures.

EPILOGUES

Expanding the Circle by Rose Borunda

Today, I call the "isms" (i.e., racism, sexism, classism, heterosexism, etc.) that exist in our society, the *smog* that clouds our vision and hinders our capacity to clearly see one another. The way in which I have seen the "ism" of racism manifested in my day-to-day life can be as innocuous as not being invited to social gatherings. In this case, I wouldn't even know that I wasn't invited but the isolation, alone, speaks volumes. This only means that I have learned to purposefully find those people with good hearts to surround me. With them, I don't have to be myself (i.e., speaking Spanish, wearing "ethnic" clothes, jewelry, etc.) out of defiance. I can be myself because I acknowledge who I am and value the *cultura* I have inherited.

Arriving to this place of consciousness has not been easy, as I have described in my last story of this book. The journey has been difficult trying to make sense of a chaotic world of inequality. There were those who busted down doors so I could be the "first one" to walk through them. Nonetheless, it hasn't all been a "homecoming parade." I have learned that people with good hearts exist in all groups. You just have to find them and be open to them. They *see* you. They care and value you. They will reach out and open doors when and where they can. On the other end, I have also come across people even from my own ethnic group who would just as easily, like the labor camp owner from my first narrative, give you "dog food" if it meant them getting ahead at your expense. It has been a journey in which I envision that we, despite the years of oppression, expand our circle and models of inclusiveness that value all people, their cultures, their languages, on *equal terms*. Like the crowd of students that had surrounded me in my high school senior year, people, who in heart, perceived that their Reina can be anyone. It can be you. . .

I have learned from those who came before me, and acknowledge that their struggles were much more difficult than mine. They did not have the opportunities or the privilege to even decide whether or not to retain their cultural identity, which is the process of cultural colonization. Their immediate focus was on survival and on ensuring that future generations came out from under. Their long-term vision, however, has made it so that the little girl who could not keep her butt in a seat, who spoke Spanish out of defiance, would ultimately reclaim the public spaces and places where she was not and continues to not always be accepted. Nonetheless, we forge ahead and evolve because *change is possible*; my father now sees the value in education and openly supports my daughter who attends a private college that is on the opposite side of this Nation. And, while the Homecoming Portrait never made it up to the collection of portraits of those who had been voted in previous to my year, you can easily find the pictures in the yearbook. Furthermore, my adult portrait, taken when I was voted in as a "Graduate of Distinction" from my high school is now displayed prominently in one of the administrative offices of the school district in my home town.

But my being the first to walk through doors is not where it ends. What I have learned is that it is my responsibility to open the door for others to pass through. It is my charge to contribute to the healing of wounded souls. And beyond this, I must ensure that *the truths imbedded in "Speaking from the Heart: Herstories of Chicana, Latina, and Amerindian Women" be told and heard by future generations.*

Deconstructing the Circle by Melissa Moreno

It is over 50 years since the Civil Rights Act was enacted into law and about 40 years since Ethnic Studies was founded to culturally decolonize our schools and society. We still have much work to do in deconstructing the master narrative that is presented as the universal truth; yet it excludes so many. In January 2012, an Ethnic Studies book banning took place with the passage of House Bill 2281 in Arizona. Even in the "progressive" state of California, there are threats to cut or remove Ethnic Studies courses or programs from our colleges or to even block Ethnic Studies books from our libraries. The dominant culture fights to protect its power, canon, and reputation as holder of the universal truth through a master narrative. When we don't understand how the context is socially constructed through the master narrative, there is no way of changing it.

Ethnic Studies texts, including this one, encourage life-long learning of a better understanding of our personal histories within a much greater context of colonialism. Ethnic Studies texts aim to represent our multicultural society; they are tools to interrogate power and structures of inequality. Through these texts, we can deconstruct the master narrative that normalizes inequalities in schools and society, resources, and political power. By reading more Ethnic Studies books, we can deconstruct the master narrative, the history we have often been taught in schools and society. In this process, we can recognize and more significantly understand the layers that exist in rich and complex cultural narratives that are woven into our identity formation and that inform our practices in everyday life. This deconstruction is essential to understanding why and how we, the present generation, are positioned today.

ABOUT THE AUTHORS

Rose Borunda is a professor in the College of Education at California State University, Sacramento. She teaches in the Master of Science in Counselor Education program where she served a four-year term as Department Chair. She also serves as Core Faculty in the Doctorate in Educational Leadership program. Her early professional experiences in the child abuse prevention field and additional years serving as a public school counselor have developed her interest in social justice. As a teacher/learner/consultant in a host of Native communities and circles through D-Q University, a tribal college, the University of California, and Davis Tribal TANF program, she has gained unique opportunities to learn orientations and perspectives not commonly heard. Her background, training, and multicultural awareness have led to publications in the areas of positive identity development, social justice, and cross-racial bridge building. Her first book, *What is the Color of Your Heart?*, promotes these capacities. The value of learning from her "first teachers," namely, her own Elders from her family and from the wider community, has been a major source of inspiration in her work. She continues to enjoy each day on this earth with her life partner, Mike, and celebrate the blessings of her two biological children, Michael and Lilian, as well as the many family and friends in her life.

Melissa Moreno grew up in the Westside of the San Joaquin Valley. She teaches and researches in the areas of Ethnic Studies, Multicultural Education, and Chicano/Latino Studies. She earned a Bachelor's degree in Sociology and in Women Studies at University of California, Santa Cruz. Then she earned a doctorate from the Education, Culture, and Society Department at University of Utah. She has taught at the University of California, Davis, and University of San Francisco. Currently, Dr. Moreno leads the Ethnic Studies program at Woodland Community College and teaches Chicana/o Studies, History of Race and Ethnicity, Mexican American History, and North American Native History. She is a former community educator and faculty in Chicana/o Studies, Education, and Liberal Studies. Her past publications have addressed issues surrounding citizenship identity, racial formation, alternative knowledge, cultural studies, and practices of young adult community-based leadership. Currently Dr. Moreno is working towards bring the topic of food justice into Ethnic Studies and she collaborates with organizations on educational programs and cultural activities for youth and young adults.

ABOUT THE CONTRIBUTORS

Margarita Ines Berta-Avila is a professor in the College of Education at Sacramento State University. She received her doctorate in International and Multicultural Education in the School of Education at the University of San Francisco. She majored as an undergraduate in Chicano Studies from the University of California, Davis, and earned her M.A. in Education and a teaching credential from Claremont Graduate University. Dr. Berta-Avila taught for seven years in the public school system, third to twelfth grades. Her area of emphasis was bilingual education. Currently, Dr. Berta-Avila teaches in the Bilingual/Multicultural Education Department. Through the Department, she teaches courses on English language learners, curriculum development/classroom management, and social political foundations in education. Dr. Berta-Avila is active in testifying at the Capitol and/or other venues with respect to access and equity in education for English Language Learners, students of color, and/or other marginalized communities. In addition, Dr. Berta-Avila pursues her scholarly work within the areas of bilingual education/English Language learners, critical pedagogy/ multicultural/social justice education, Chicana/o educators in the field, qualitative research, and language usage. In collaboration with Dr. Julie Figueroa and Dr. Anita Tijerina-Revilla, an edited volume titled *Marching Students: Chicana/o Activism in Education, 1968 to the Present* was released this past spring of 2011.

Angie Chabram is a professor in the Department of Chicana/o Studies at the University of California, Davis. She edited *The Chicana/o Cultural Studies Reader* and *The Chicana/o Cultural Studies Forum*. Also she coedited *Speaking from the Body: Latinas on Health and Culture* with Adela de la Torre. She is from La Puente, California.

Cindy Cruz is an assistant professor in the Department of Education at the University of California, Santa Cruz. She is an interdisciplinary scholar with a background in both humanities and in social sciences, with

149

Chicano/Latino Studies, Anthropology, and Education as her disciplines. Cruz's research begins as a reexamination of the writings of U.S. Third World feminists, locating the queer brown body as central in an ongoing practice of negotiation in which multiple, often opposing, ideas and ways of being are addressed, appropriated, and negotiated. Through interviews, direct and participant observations, and the close readings of student video and photographic narrative, Cruz find that the queer body, fragmented by multiple identities and subjectivities, serves the purpose of deconstructing the racialized and gendered discourses inscripted upon young LGBTQ students. Cindy Cruz was selected as the recipient of the 2012 Article of the Year award by the Queer Studies Special Interest Group of the American Educational Research Association (AERA). One of her many publications is entitled "LGBTQ street youth talk back: A meditation on resistance and witnessing."

Julie López Figueroa is currently an associate professor at California State University, Sacramento in the Department of Ethnic Studies. Prior to this academic position, Dr. Figueroa completed her doctoral studies in Education from the University of California, Berkeley, in 2002, completed her M.A. in Education in 1995 from the University of California, Santa Cruz, and her B.A. in Sociology and Chicana/o Studies from the University of California, Davis. Areas of scholarly interest include qualitative research methods, access and retention in higher education, and teaching and learning in a cultural context. Dr. Figueroa actively works at local, state, and national levels with scholars, policymakers, and community organizations to increase the access and success of Chican@/Latin@s in higher education.

Marcela S. Jáuregui earned her Bachelor's degree in Sociocultural Anthropology from the University of California, Davis. As a first-generation college graduate, she aspires to pursue a career in teaching to inspire students to realize their dreams through education.

Jennie Luna was born and raised in East San José, California. Granddaughter/daughter of migrant farm workers and cannery workers, she is the first in her family to attend and graduate from college. She received her B.A. in Chicana/o Studies and Mass Communications from the University of California, Berkeley; Master's in Education from Teachers College, Columbia University; and a Ph.D. in Native American Studies from the University of California, Davis. Her research focuses on the contemporary history of Danza Mexica/Azteca tradition and the diaspora of Danza in the United States. Her dissertation is titled "La Danza Mexica: Native Identity, Spirituality, Activism, and Performance." Dr. Luna's research incorporates Nahuatl language study, representations of indigeneity, and the role of women in Intercontinental and global Native movements. She has worked as both scholar and community organizer in Northern California and New York City and as cofounder of Calpulli Cetiliztli Nauhcampa Quetzalcoatl Danza circle and La Red Xicana Indígena international network. Currently, she is an Assistant Professor at California State University, Channel Island.

Michelle Maher is an assistant professor in the Graduate School at Lewis & Clark College in Portland, Oregon. She is an advocate for youth and an educator and activist. She is interested in schools that are communities, the social construction of difference, liberatory education, and living in balance. She thanks all that have helped her and those who have kept sacred traditions going. She thanks you for recognizing that your efforts have a legacy. She prays to live in service of those blessings and wisdom she has received. She is so grateful for walking the Red Road that has many other footprints along it. She thanks the Creator for leaving the answer in our own hearts and acknowledges that we may all live in balance.

Maria Mejorado is an associate professor in the College of Education at California State University, Sacramento, and former Director of the High School Equivalency Program (HEP), a federally funded GED preparation program for seasonal agricultural workers. Maria was born in the Central San Joaquin Valley as the last of seven siblings and the only daughter. Her family's livelihood depended on harvesting grapes, peaches, and oranges and working in the local packing houses. Her earliest recollection of contributing to the family income was picking cotton and grapes at age four. School proved to be the answer to breaking the cycle of poverty. As the first member of her family, Maria earned a Bachelor's degree from St. Mary's College, a Master's degree from Harvard University, and Doctorate at UC Davis. At CSUS, she teaches undergraduate and graduate students and those pursuing a teaching credential. Her research interests include mentoring, parent involvement, teaching and learning of seasonal agricultural adults and its impact on their children.

Rebecca Rosa is a lecturer and university supervisor in the Social Science Credential Program in the School of Education at the University of California, Davis.

Caroline Sotello Viernes Turner is a professor of Doctorate in Educational Leadership and Policy Studies, California State University, Sacramento, and Lincoln Professor Emerita of Ethics and Education, Arizona State University. She is the recipient of two American Educational Research Association (AERA) Distinguished Career and Lifetime Scholarship awards and an Exemplary Scholarship award from the Association for the Study of Higher Education (ASHE) Council for Ethnic Participation.

Turner received her doctorate in Administration and Policy Analysis from the Stanford University School of Education.

Ruth Trinidad-Galván is an associate professor of Educational Thought and Sociocultural Studies in the Language, Literacy, and Sociocultural Studies Department at the University of New Mexico. Dr. Trinidad-Galván received her Ph.D. from the University of Utah, where she focused her research with rural Mexican women. It is now published in Spanish [Relatos de Supervivencia: Desafíos y bienestar en unacomunidadtransmigrante Mexicana]. Raised in East Los Angeles, she was an adult ESL instructor and Bilingual Educator in inner city schools in California. She is a Fulbright Scholar, recipient of an AERA/Spencer Fellowship, associate editor of the Journal of Latinos and Education and coeditor of the Handbook of Latinos and Education. Her research foci include gendered analyses of global, transnational and migration issues; popular education; transborder feminist epistemologies and pedagogies; and qualitative research in education.

Sofia Villenas is an associate professor in the Department of Anthropology and Director of the Latino Studies Program at Cornell University. She was born and raised in Los Angeles, a daughter of immigrant parents from Ecuador. Her teaching experiences as an adult educator and as a Spanish bilingual schoolteacher in Los Angeles inspired her to pursue a doctoral degree from the University of North Carolina at Chapel Hill with a focus on the social, cultural, and political dimensions of education. She is coeditor of *Race is . . . Race isn't: Critical Race Theory and Qualitative Studies in Education* (with L. Parker and D. Deyhle, 1999), *Chicana/Latina Education in Everyday Life* (with D. Delgado Bernal, C. A. Elenes, and F. Godinez), and most recently, the *Handbook of Latinos and Education: Theory, Research, and Practice* (with E. Murillo Jr., R. Trinidad-Galvan, J. Muñoz, C. Martinez, and M. Machado-Casas, 2010). She is a mother of three sons and one daughter and lives in Ithaca, New York.

CHAPTER DISCUSSION QUESTIONS

Chapter 1

Analytical Questions

1. How does Borunda's narrative describe educational and social inequality? In what way was inequality "normalized" in her schooling and society?
2. Compare and contrast the primary and secondary schooling conditions in Borunda's narrative. How does Borunda's access to college preparatory and extracurricular activity become important to her college aspirations?
3. How does Borunda's narrative describe her process of entering college and her first year experiences? Discuss what cultural challenges she faced with her family and her peers at a predominantly "white" educational institution.

Self-Reflection Questions

1. Discuss how and what you have learned about your family's labor history. What were the labor struggles and in what ways did they offer social mobility or opportunities to you, your family, and community?
2. Were you able to access college preparatory and extracurricular activities? If so, in what ways and what were the implications? Give three examples. If not, how so?
3. What was your first year college experience like, with regard to how others viewed your ethnicity and class? Who was perceived as belonging or not belonging in college? Did you create a social network of peers; if so, how?

Chapter 2

Analytical Questions

1. How does Borunda's narrative describe her family migrations within a U.S.–Mexican context?
2. How does Borunda's narrative describe generational differences in terms of the different opportunities afforded to different family members?

3. Borunda ends her narrative by stating, ". . . here we are and here we belong." Explain what she means and how she acquires a sense of belonging in society.

Self-Reflection Questions

1. Discuss how and what you were taught about your own family's migration or immigration history. What historical event(s) in society shaped their personal histories of migration or immigration?
2. Discuss what you have learned about the generational differences in your family's history. Why or why not have they experienced social mobility or opportunities in schools and society?
3. Has your family acquired a sense of belonging in this society? If so, in what ways have they or have they not formed a sense of belonging? Give three examples?

Chapter 3

Analytical Questions

1. What is colonization and what is decolonization? How does Borunda's narrative directly characterize colonization and indirectly describe decolonization? Give examples.
2. How are Borunda's grandparents' impacted by categories of race and class, as constructed during the colonial era?
3. What are the implications of colonial history on the status of Borunda's Grandfather Hermann? Explain his situation with the landowner and the duel match and how Spanish masculine culture impacted him.

Self-Reflection Questions

1. Have you or your family experienced de/colonization? If so, in what ways? Give three examples. If not, why so?
2. How have you learned about the "discovery" of the Americas and Native peoples? Give three examples. What are the stereotypes that may be associated to these narratives? If not, why so?
3. What kinds of values and beliefs have you been socialized with in regards to race and class categories. Who is described as belonging or not belonging in your family, community, or society, due to class or skin color? What are the implications?

Chapter 4

Analytical Questions

1. What is the difference between the notions of contact, invasion, conquest, colonization, and decolonization? What connotations and notions of power and authority do each of these terms imply? Give examples.

2. What does Borunda's narrative convey about the Mexica and how and why have they come to represent the conditions and status of many Native People of Mexico?

3. How does Borunda's narrative describe the significance of Elder Mama Cobb and her world view? How does Elder Mama Cobb's world view counter the master narrative?

4. What are the cultural symbols or ceremonial items and practices that help Borunda and her daughter connect to a Native cultural awareness and identity? How or why can the coming of age ceremony be described as a transcultural (syncretism or hybrid) Native offering?

Self-Reflection Questions

1. Have you learned about Native or other cultural groups outside of your own? If so, what are some appropriate and non-appropriate ways? Give four examples. If not, why not?

2. Were you taught about Native people and culture as something of the past or as living entities today? If so, in what ways? Give three examples. If not, how so? Describe the differences between learning about Native people as something of the past or as living entities of today.

3. Do you have cultural symbols or practices that connect you to a cultural identity and awareness? If so, in what ways? Give three examples. If not, what symbols or practices do you do?

4. Are "coming of age" and "rites of passage ceremonies" significant for your cultural identity formation and community building? If so, in what ways? Give examples. If not, why so?

CPSIA information can be obtained
at www.ICGtesting.com
Printed in the USA
LVOW02s0932080517
533072LV00004B/7/P